YOUR GOD IS HERE AND NOW

IN MEMORY OF
JENNIFER

YOUR GOD IS HERE AND NOW

J.B. Phillips

Guildford, Surrey

British Library Cataloguing-in-Publication Data. A catalogue record for this book is available from the British Library.

First published in 1960 as *God our Contemporary*, by Hodder & Stoughton Limited. This edition, published with the permission of the trustees of the estate of J.B. Phillips, is published in 1997 by Eagle, an imprint of Inter Publishing Service (IPS) Ltd, St Nicholas House, 14 The Mount, Guildford, Surrey GU2 5HN.

Typeset by Palimpsest Book Production Limited, Polmont, Stirlingshire
Printed in the UK by Cox & Wyman Ltd, Reading, Berkshire.

ISBN: 086347 218 4

CONTENTS

PREFACE

This book was first published as *God our Contemporary* in 1960, but the reader will quickly discover that it is as relevant today as it was when first written.

J.B. Phillips was the pioneer of that post-war movement of translations of the Bible into 'Today's English'. He was essentially a communicator, who will always be remembered for his ability to let the New Testament speak in the language we use day by day. His translations and his books of spiritual guidance were a success beyond his imagining. But he paid a price for that success, as he describes in his autobiography, *The Price of Success:*

> I was in a state of excitement throughout the whole of 1955. My work hardly seemed arduous for it was intrinsically exciting. I was tasting the sweets of success to an almost unimaginable degree. My health was excellent, my future prospects were rosier than my wildest dreams could ever suggest; applause, honour and appreciation met me wherever I went . . . I was not aware of the dangers of success. The subtle corrosion of character, the unconscious changing of values, and the secret monstrous growth of a vastly inflated idea of myself seeped slowly into me. Vaguely, I was aware of this, and like some frightful parody of St Augustine, I prayed, 'Lord, make me humble – but not yet.'

In the late summer of 1961, the crisis came. Quite suddenly, his cherished powers of speaking, writing and communicating stopped. Although he did do some writing after this and even translated four prophetic books from the Old Testament, the old sense of power had gone.

As a kind of compensation, he developed a great compassion for those who suffered. His parish became a vast correspondence. What he had written had helped so many people that they wrote to him with their doubts and distress and every letter he answered with the sure touch of a pastor. Some of those letters are published in *The Wounded Healer*, which his widow and I published about the same time as his autobiography. Many of the letters, published and unpublished, referred to *God our Contemporary*.

A woman from Canada wrote: 'I have just concluded reading your wonderful book, *God our Contemporary*. I am truly convinced that God is giving you insight and knowledge of his ways and plans, that few others have.' As a result, she was able to share with him problems of faith and her relationship with a husband who had given up the Christian faith for a virulent form of atheism. With great commonsense and with that clarity which marks all his writings, he began a correspondence with her which led to reconciliation. Her last letter concludes, 'I shall be forever grateful for your kindness and your sympathy at a trying time in my life.'

Several of the letters deal with the effect of psychiatry on faith and J.B. Phillips clearly seemed to be able to help those whose faith was shattered to recover, not their childish religion, but a mature faith.

In 1969, he received a letter from a man who had been greatly impressed by Aldous Huxley's *Perennial Philosophy*, but was brought up short when he read *God our Contemporary*. He wrote: 'I am at present reading your *God our Contemporary* and have reached chapter 8.' He then quoted Phillips as saying that it is impossible to compile a religion for modern man from the best elements in all religions. In correspondence, the argument continued based upon a careful reading of chapter 8, 'Religion and Modern Knowledge'. Although science has moved on since 1969, that chapter still holds its own against the most seductive forms of eclecticism.

A church in Cheshire had been using J.B. Phillips' books for some time in study groups and were looking for another when someone suggested *God our Contemporary*. One of the group leaders wrote to say how perfectly it fitted their need:

> After New Year, our PCC is circularizing the parish with a questionnaire on stewardship in its widest sense, on churchgoing and people's various reasons for non-attendance and lack of interest. The PCC members have pledged themselves to help the clergy in following up requests for personal discussion about it. Many of us feel ill-equipped for such a task, but *God our Contemporary* gave marvellous help on the whole subject.

That particular writer said, 'Don't answer, get on with your valuable work.' Others kept up a continuous correspondence for years. Reading it through, I am most aware of the integrity of J.B. Phillips, standing by the statements he had made, explaining they were necessary and trying, as always, to clear people's minds of preconceived ideas, hardening into prejudice. He believed, and shows most clearly in this book, that the Christian faith is defensible in the modern world.

How very perceptive was the PS in one letter he received: 'It must be a true satisfaction that through your work of several years ago you are still helping people like us – ordinary people though they be – and in your books there's so much of your own personal faith which helps me enormously.'

A retired minister in 1968 commended the book for its 'sane and practical value' and urged J.B. Phillips to call the leaders of the church together to represent the Christian faith in just such a way as the book does: 'I do most definitely agree that the true vital faith needs to be represented by every means possible to the people of this land of ours.'

There are scores of letters from people stimulated by the penultimate chapter 20, 'Representing Christianity'. By then, Phillips could do little more than answer the letters, and allowing his writing to stimulate, keep up a voluminous correspondence. He was himself in a deep clinical depression.

Edwin Robertson
Hampstead, January 1997

Chapter One

THE TIME IN WHICH WE LIVE

The concern of this present book is chiefly the relationship of man with the contemporary God, and it is in this context particularly important not to sigh for old days which can never come back. If we admit the existence of 'God' we can certainly claim that because of his nature the passage of time cannot alter his character. But as for man, his conditions of life, his perceptions and outlook, his attitude of mind, both towards himself and towards any possible Creator, have all changed so enormously this century that we face almost a new situation. In the whole long history of mankind there has never been such a violent acceleration in the acquisition of human knowledge, at least of certain kinds. We really cannot be surprised that the young person of today is very largely lacking in historical sense. There is such a fundamental difference between his attitude to life and that of his counterpart of less than a hundred years ago, that he can hardly be blamed if he sees no more than the most tenuous connection between his own age and all the previous centuries.

This marked change of outlook has swept over us with unbelievable speed. It is in a really very tiny fraction of the thousands of years of recorded human history that the lonely watcher on the hill has been superseded by scanning radar, the cannonball by the guided missile, the urgent message on horseback by the telephone call, the peepshow by the cinema, the spreading of unreliable rumour by responsible broadcasting, the eye-witness account given to a few by the mass-perception of television, the months-long weary voyage by quick and comfortable transport, dangerous and arduous labour by powerful electronic devices. New fabrics, new materials included under the general term of 'plastics', new drugs and antibiotics, the mechanisation of farm and factory labour, new methods of food-packing and the widespread use of refrigeration, these and a hundred more things are quite new in the human scene. It is no good repeating nowadays the weary old cliché, 'there is nothing new under the sun', for it is obviously and demonstrably untrue. There are literally thousands of human discoveries and devices which have never, even in embryo, appeared before in human life.

In addition to this, never in all our human history has there been such interchange between the nations not only of ideas but of living people. (We need constantly to remember that in past centuries only a very privileged or adventurous few were able to travel at all.) The network of news-coverage throughout the world is so efficient, and on the whole so reliable, that the intelligent man of today may make himself better informed about events in the distant places of the world than the intelligent man only a hundred years ago could make himself informed about events within his own country. Despite all our fears and prejudices and differences, it is for the first time becoming possible for thinking people to sense what was foreseen a long time ago, that we are 'members one of another'.

Yet while human achievement in practical and scientific matters has progressed by leaps and bounds, the presentation of the Christian religion is still frequently made in an atmosphere at once stuffy and old-fashioned. The language of many hymns, is unquestionably heavily redolent of the past, only partially aware of the present and vaguely hopeful about the future. At the risk of offending many Christian people it has to be said that to the impartial observer, the faithful Christian is apparently saying, 'This must be true, it has been believed for so many centuries.' But the non-Christian is at least sometimes saying, 'This thing may be essentially true, but it is so old and encrusted by tradition that it is high time that it was cleaned and re-examined.' Under sentimental appeals, under pressures of guilt or fear, through a wistful nostalgia for the serenity and security of the past, or in sheer desperation through his modern bewilderment, modern man may be driven to accept the faith and trappings of past ages. But for every one who consents to do this, there are a dozen people of goodwill who cannot be intellectually dishonest, who cannot lightly forget the fears and superstitions of the past, and who cannot reconcile what appears to them to be the mumbo-jumbo of bygone days with the clear cold knowledge of the present. If there is a God at all he must be 'big enough' to fit into the modern scene (and that naturally means a conception of the Creator a million times greater than that held even a century ago).

Although we are deeply concerned with the present and the future, no sensible person will deny his debt to the past. If it is impossible to put back the clock, it is equally impossible to think that we can face life today without the slightest regard for the generations which have preceded us. It is neither more nor less than adolescent arrogance to think that any generation starts *de novo*. Young people, for example, may be intensely critical of all that has been taught them, and may be contemptuous of the tradition and culture in which they find themselves, but they would be in no position to exercise their critical faculty at all if it were not for the educational process which is part of the system they are so anxious to denigrate. Even on the purely physical plane the voluble young rebel against the present order of things owes far more than he realises to the past. What young person could feed himself, or maintain even a modest level of hygiene, without using the knowledge and accumulated experience of other people? Does he know anything about agriculture, weaving, the manufacture of soap or indeed of the mechanical processes which enable him to disseminate his ideas? I am not at all sure that this very obvious debt to the past is always clear to the modern 'clevers'. The most clear-sighted, fearless and unprejudiced writer of today is only able to do what he does because of the knowledge and invention of the generations which lie behind him. The modern writer, however contemptuous of days gone by, does not write as an Australian aborigine or a South American Indian.

Just as inescapably as we are rooted in the past, so there is a quite inevitable 'given-ness' about the present human predicament. In our rebellious adolescent days we all feel like the poet who wanted, 'to grasp this sorry Scheme of Things entire' and 'remould it nearer to the Heart's Desire'. But as we grow more mature, we realise that such a sentiment is not only highly egocentric but utterly impracticable. The plain fact is that we can do little or nothing about the basic terms on which we live life. It is only after acceptance of these terms that we can do something constructive and practical. More serious attention would be deserved by the outbursts against Things as They Are if the rebels themselves would do something more than denounce and destroy. They claim that there are no causes left to live and die for, but I have yet to hear of an angry young man dedicating his life to the cure of leprosy, to the care of crippled children or the spreading of medical knowledge in newly-awakening continents, to name but a few of the worthwhile human causes. They cry that they have nothing in which to put their faith, but have they seriously considered the claims of true Christianity? If one looks upon human life as a challenge to courage, compassion and charity, the anger could be readily transformed into worthwhile energy, the frustration be resolved and the self-pity be forgotten.

Chapter Two

FAITH AND UNFAITH

Many men and women are baffled and bewildered by the complexities of the modern human scene. They can see no sense or purpose in it at all, and many of them are not a little frightened at the new vistas of human knowledge and power which are continually opening up in a dozen different fields. Most of them hold on, without much reason or authority, to the moral standards of what is commonly supposed to be the good life. But it must be plainly said that when they turn to the churches they feel they are entering the atmosphere of a bygone age. Indeed the whole language, teaching and climate of 'Church' appears almost totally irrelevant to modern life. I am not of course saying that the irrelevancy is factual. I am merely concerned to point out that this is how the whole machinery of 'Church' often appears to the outsider.

I am happy to be aware of exceptions, but the fact remains that most of the practising Christians in our churches are the product of Christian parents – there is a sort of hereditary indoctrination. What is more, almost every clergyman or minister of my acquaintance comes from a Christian family, and is not infrequently 'a son of the manse'. The training of young men for the ministry of the Church is certainly far better today than it was when I myself was ordained. Nevertheless, I am convinced that even today it does not do enough to help a man understand the unbelieving world to which he is called to minister. It is not uncommon to find that those who train him, however learned they may be in such matters as theology and Church history, are almost totally ignorant of non-Christian ways of thinking except perhaps theoretically. It is still possible to find plenty of ordained men who have never worked, in the secular sense, in the contemporary world, and who find it difficult to understand the perplexity and insecurity of godless materialism. The very fact that the modern Church finds 'communication' such a desperately difficult problem is undeniable evidence of its lack of understanding of the world of un-faith. I know that these are hard words, but they are not written in any spirit of useless criticism. I am merely concerned to point out, and to emphasise as strongly as I can, what is to me the daily tragedy – the gulf between the good men of faith and the good men of unfaith. Let us put briefly the two contemporary points of view.

The Christian believes in a God of Love, All-powerful and All-wise. He believes man to be God's special creation, and whether he believes the fault to derive from the failure of the first man or not, he believes mankind to be suffering from a universal infection called 'sin'. He is inclined to believe that the non-apprehension of God is chiefly due to this moral infection. The Christian further believes that the eventual effect of sin is death, and that man would be in a hopeless *impasse* were it not for God's personal visit to this earth in the man Jesus Christ. This man not only provided a perfect example of human living but by making himself, as it were, representative man, allowed the forces of evil to close in upon him and kill him. By this action he reconciled the sinful human race with the utter perfection and holiness of God. After his death by crucifixion he returned to life again, both to prove his own claim to be divine, and to demonstrate the fact that he had overcome the power of death. After his Resurrection and Ascension he sent his own Spirit into the personalities of his early followers so that they might be the spearhead of a movement designed to convert the world to belief in, and co-operation with, God himself. Christians further believe that Jesus Christ founded a Church which is to be on earth a witness to heavenly truth, and that he gave that Church unique spiritual authority. The Church therefore seeks to add to its membership so that men and women may be reconciled with God and may do his will upon earth.

In sharp contrast with this view of life is that of the intelligent agnostic. He finds himself part of a vast number of human beings living on this comparatively tiny planet. He knows something of the aeons of time which must have elapsed before *homo sapiens* appeared. He can probably see an upward trend in the process of evolution, however blind and ruthless that process may sometimes seem to be. But, if he is honest, he is not wholly convinced that the present tendencies of man are in an upward direction. He cannot help observing evil, injustice and cruelty. He cannot help seeing how frequently the innocent suffer and how the tough and cruel go through life comparatively unscathed. He also sees a good deal of human unselfishness, kindness and courage, and these qualities he is prepared to recognise as good and even to regard with a certain reverence. Now the Christian's starting-point, or at least the starting-point of such evangelism as he may chance to hear, probably seems to him quite monstrous. The emphasis is on human sin and on the failure of men to reach the apparently arbitrary standards of God. After all, he thinks, if there is a God in charge of the whole bewildering universe, it seems singularly unfair that he should be presented in the role of a hanging judge! For, to put it plainly, he holds all the cards and knows all the answers, while even the most devout Christian, on his own admission, walks by faith and not by sight. It seems to our sensitive agnostic that the God presented by the passionate evangelist is making unwarrantable demands. For if, after a long process of evolution, highly complex beings with self-consciousness emerge, then surely any reasonable Creator would not expect too much of his creatures who are blind and limited through no fault of their own. Indeed, if there is a God his attitude towards man could fairly be expected to show both pity and the desire to help. But to call his creatures 'sinners', and to insist that to admit their 'sin' is the only way to get to know him, seems uncomfortably like condemning a small child for not understanding the binomial theorem!

To my mind the difference between these two points of view is not always properly appreciated. The Christian, who is far more indoctrinated than he realises by upbringing and training, very naturally tends to consort with fellow-Christians who share his point of view. If he is a clergyman or minister his specialised training will condition him even more deeply. It becomes virtually impossible for him to view the human scene without theological colour. He holds a faith which, in my view, is infinitely worth passing on; he is more often than not a man of kindness, compassion and sympathy. But again and again he feels frustrated and grows disheartened because he does not really understand the thinking and feeling of people who possess absolutely nothing of that Christian conviction which shapes his whole life.

At the same time the intelligent agnostic, with his prejudices against the churches and all their ways, very rarely takes the trouble to look behind the tradition and the façade and to find out the meaning of essential Christianity. His knowledge of what the alert modern Church is doing in any part of the world is usually infinitesimal, and equally minute is his first-hand adult knowledge of the early Christian documents which comprise the New Testament. Consequently his attacks on the churches are nearly always ill-informed or out of date. If he rarely fires a shot at Christianity itself it is simply because he usually has little more than a very sketchy knowledge of what it is all about.

There is an added difficulty in the modern situation which is not always appreciated by the sincere lifelong Christian. In the old days, when man knew very little about the true nature of the physical world, he could very easily be reduced to a state of awe and even terror by natural phenomena which he did not understand. But with the vast increase in scientific knowledge this century a knowledge which is expanding all the time – man's attitude towards Nature has greatly changed. When confronted with the inexplicable his reaction is very far from that of the saints of old who could humbly say, 'It is the Lord, let him do what seemeth to him good.' Old-fashioned humility of this kind is a very delightful virtue, especially when we observe it in other people's lives! But the modern agnostic is not necessarily lacking in humility when his reaction before the inexplicable is markedly different. He says in effect, 'This is something new to human experience; let us try to understand it and, if possible, control it.' And it may be worth pointing out here that if it were not for this attitude men would still be living in terror of darkness, lightning and contagious disease.

Some Christians, at least, do not appear to have properly observed this change of atmosphere in thinking. For a man who believes in a God who is a benevolent Heavenly Father, it may be easy to accept life at the Father's hand. But it is really expecting too much to think that the intelligent agnostic is going to smother his own critical faculty and observations of life and submit to an unknown quantity called 'the Lord's will'. The modern agnostic, who is by no means unaware of the mystery of life, is not nearly so arrogant as he appears. But he is not going to be shocked or coerced into faith by the sheer weight of the inexplicable. 'If we admit that there is a God,' he is saying, 'surely we can consider ourselves as having passed the fears and bogeys of childhood. Cannot God treat us as intelligent adults and let us have at least a few hints as to what life is all about? Can we not know something of its purpose so that we may co-operate with it? We cannot abrogate our intelligence, but we would give a great deal to have reliable clues to the nature and purpose of life.' Surely such an attitude is reasonable, and surely the Christian should try to understand it!

Chapter Three

A PLEA FOR UNDERSTANDING

I have already mentioned the widespread ignorance on both sides of the chasm which divides the world and the Church. The traditional churches do not always seem to realise that the premises for sensible argument, which are basic to themselves, are probably neither valid nor comprehensible in the world outside the Church. When the practising Christian talks to modern man about the 'Law of God', the 'Teaching of the Church', or invokes the authority of Holy Scripture, he is to his own mind bringing out the heaviest weapons in his armoury. But to the man whose idea of God is nebulous to the point of negligibility the invocation of 'God's Law' is quite meaningless. To say that 'the Church teaches' is equally without force, for the man of intelligence knows, in the first place, that there are a great many churches and that some of their teaching is contradictory. Secondly, he may ask rudely but pertinently, 'Who are the churches, anyway, and by what right do they attempt to speak with authority to me?' And although in the heated atmosphere of the revival meeting the phrase 'the Bible says' may carry fervent conviction, the intelligent man who has read the Bible knows perfectly well that it can be made to 'say' a lot of things, and that, as a matter of sober history, witch-hunting, slave-owning and the inhuman policy of apartheid have all been justified by reference to the same Bible.

But the ignorance and misunderstanding does not exist only on the side of professing Christians. There is, for example, a basic misconception held by a great many people outside the Christian Church. It is commonly supposed that, in the religious view, life is primarily a kind of competition in goodness and morality! Consequently, the agnostic who can, and frequently does say, 'I am as good as So-and-so who goes to church,' feels that he has given a final and unanswerable reply to the whole Christian position! But true Christianity has never taught that life is primarily a kind of competition in goodness. Most Christians today are 'in the Church' because they have felt the need for God and for co-operating with what they know of his purpose. There probably were times in the history of the Christian Church in this country when some churchgoing Christians would look upon themselves as 'superior' to those outside the Church. But to imagine that such is the common attitude today would be laughable if it were not a tragic part of the misunderstanding between the worlds of faith and unfaith. Most modern churchgoers give their weekly witness to their own inner conviction without the slightest sense of being superior, and more frequently than is sometimes supposed, it is given by young Christians despite ridicule, discouragement and even some persecution. If I plead for more understanding on the part of Christians for those who have not enjoyed a Christian upbringing, I would also plead that the agnostic should know much more accurately than he appears to do what the Christians of today, particularly the young Christians, really believe.

Now apart from the nonsense of the supposed 'competition in goodness' both Christians and humanists believe that it is important to lead a good life. But in this country there is not the sharp black-and-white contrast between Christians and pagans, largely, I believe, because the whole life of the country has been soaked for many centuries in the Christian tradition. Thousands of people today are exhibiting, even to a marked degree, 'the fruits of the Spirit' which Paul listed long ago in his letter to Galatia. They are, for the record, 'love, joy, peace, patience, kindness, generosity, fidelity, tolerance and self-control'.

It is obvious that these qualities are no monopoly of the churches, and that devoted selfless service is quite frequently given without any religious faith. It is naturally argued by our scientific humanists that this is good and normal human behaviour. But is this really so? It would need first-hand knowledge of an entirely pagan country to say for certain that these impressive spiritual qualities are growing spontaneously, rather than being the delayed action of many years of unconscious Christian absorption. It could surely be reasonably argued that many people in this country are living on the spiritual capital of the past, and that there are signs that the capital is being depleted. Already there are many thousands of present-day parents who were brought up with no religious faith and few standards, and they have had almost nothing, and sometimes less than nothing of spiritual value, to pass on to their children. Surely it is not far-fetched to suggest that the depletion of spiritual capital accounts for the breakdown of moral standards in our society. For, as I hope to show in a later chapter, moral standards ultimately depend upon something transcending the human scene.

Quite apart from the gulf between the comparatively small world of faith and the world of unfaith there are innumerable smaller gulfs between various sections of our common life. I am not pining for the long-past 'ages of faith' when I point out that there was in those days a communal basic belief in God and in revealed standards of human behaviour. This central belief to a large extent held people together in their widely varying activities. Moreover, in days when the sum total of human knowledge could practically be held in the mind of one man, the division caused by human specialisation was little more than a superficial difference of function. Men could at least imagine that all truth was one.

But today, in our country, the picture is entirely different. A common faith in God is held by only a minority, and comparatively few people believe that there is Absolute Truth to which all human discoveries of truth can be referred. This means in effect that our modern greatly accentuated specialisation tends to divide people more and more.

In our industralised society all kinds of professions and vocations, all kinds of skilled and unskilled occupations, tend to become wrapped in their own cocoon of specialised knowledge, and to have little more than superficial contacts outside their own mystiques. What does the steelworker, for example, know of the life and problems of a secondary modern school-teacher? What does the electronics engineer know of the life and problems of the surgeon? Such examples could obviously be multiplied many times; there are many human occupations which exist in practical isolation from the rest of the community, and in the absence of a common faith there is today no effective meeting-point. From time to time crises such as strike-action remind people that they are dependent upon one another, but for the most part they live and work within the confines of their own occupation, and there is extraordinarily little communication of ideas of any significance. This truth is most easily observed by those who have the opportunity of passing readily through the unseen barriers. The doctor, the nurse and the clergyman or minister are some of the few who can observe these divisions.

Now these people, divided into occupational compartments of knowledge, skill and experience, are a kind of parable of what is happening in the realm of thought. The scientist who is exploring the very frontiers of human knowledge in some specialised department of truth may have absolutely no knowledge of the work of any other specialist, and may indeed take a certain pride in such ignorance! Of course there is a fascination in retiring more and more completely into the ivory tower of expert knowledge, and the temptation to do so is just as real to the religious man as it is to the poet, the archaeologist, the astronomer, the geneticist, the mathematician, and all the others. But the result of such retirement is that there is no common pool of human knowledge, no interaction between various aspects of truth, and no kind of conclusion based on the total of human knowledge and experience. It will naturally be objected that the real expert cannot share his specialised knowledge with the untrained, and that is no doubt true. But surely his point of view can be expressed, and the reason for his dedication to his particular facet of truth translated into terms comprehensible to other men of intelligence? Can it not be more widely recognised that we are all in the human predicament together, and that the pooling of knowledge and experience might lead to considerably more light being shed on the business of living which faces every one of us.

There is another danger in extreme specialisation. Unless the specialist informs himself to a reasonable degree outside his speciality he can easily be misled in a department where his critical faculties have no familiar data on which to work. Thus a dedicated scientist who feels, because he is a human being, the need for something less coldly detached from humanity may easily be drawn into a religious cult which is both crude and obscurantist. His highly-developed mind apparently ceases to function in an unfamiliar milieu – or it is possible that he may not wish it to function. Psychologically it may be an enormous relief to him to enter a world of warmth and fantasy after the cold, disciplined life of the laboratory where feelings count not at all. That this can and does happen I know from personal experience, and it sometimes has unhappy consequences. For other scientists, doctors, or whatever the specialists may be, are apt to jump to the conclusion that 'religion' is simply an emotional escape. They are therefore hardly encouraged to examine such a phenomenon as Christianity with unprejudiced critical faculties.

Apart from such dangers in excessive specialisation, there is a kind of intellectual snobbery about the whole matter which I am sure all men of goodwill should steadfastly resist. I call to mind a former high dignitary of the Church of England who was presented with a fountain-pen. But he never used it, on the simple grounds that 'he did not understand mechanical things'! I cannot see why the artist should despise the engineer or the engineer the artist, and I have little patience for artists or intellectuals of one sort or another who dismiss a scientific device, which has taken years of patience to perfect, as a mere gadget. Those who make it their proud boast that they 'don't know the first thing about electricity and couldn't even mend a fuse' or, when referring to their car, say, 'I haven't the remotest idea what goes on under the bonnet, I just drive the thing', are to my mind guilty of a quite unpardonable conceit. It would not take them long to understand at least the elementary principles of those things which they affect to despise, and even to have some clue to the rudiments might give them an inkling into the enormous skill, patience and ingenuity which lie behind the practical application of physical science. Those who loudly deplore the intrusion of 'science' into our private lives and speak nostalgically of the past would be among the first to complain if they were deprived of the convenience of electric light, the telephone or the motor car! On the other hand, the man of science has no right to dismiss a religion such as Christianity, for example, as a mere hangover from more primitive days. He surely cannot seriously imagine that men of similar intellectual calibre to his own have not asked the same searching fundamental questions about life and its meaning which he himself asks, and yet have come to the conclusion that the Christian faith is an indispensable part of total truth. If it is rare to find a bishop, shall we say, giving time and thought to understand the elements of a scientific process, it is, in my experience at least, also rare to find a scientist giving his serious attention to the meaning and significance of Christianity.

Obviously, in an age such as ours there must be specialisation; but must there be such drastic isolation of objective? Surely there need not be such divisive walls between art, science and religion, erected and maintained only too often by pride, ignorance and prejudice. No intelligent seeker after truth imagines that he is the only one on the right track, and the time has gone by when complete ignorance of another man's point of view could be considered a virtue.

Chapter Four

THE INADEQUACY OF HUMANISM

The prevailing atmosphere among thinking men and women of goodwill today is one of what may loosely be termed 'scientific humanism'. Since all of us are filled with admiration for the achievements of science, and since all of us desire to practise and propagate such human virtues as friendliness, tolerance, good humour, sympathy and courage, we unconsciously assent to scientific humanism as a working philosophy of life. What we do not so readily see is that science has very little to offer in solving problems of human relationships, even though these are the problems which most need to be solved. Nor do we see, behind what appears to be a kind-hearted philosophy, an utter denial of any dimension beyond this present observable life, of any such thing as absolute right or wrong and of any power which might be called God.

Now although I know that many humanists are good and kind people I remain convinced that humanism itself is a bleak and cruel creed. For it offers man a blank denial where his needs are greatest and his aspirations frequently most desperate. But before we examine this failure let us see the extraordinarily fragile foundation upon which the humanist position rests. No man in this country with its centuries-old tradition of Christianity can detach himself from that tradition, however vehemently he abuses the Christian faith and denies the existence of God. Not all humanists, of course, are to be found attacking Christianity or denying God; many of them indeed strike me as wistful people. But humanism itself, according to its official literature, explicitly denies the Christian faith and the need for any moral or spiritual authority outside humanity.

What exactly does humanism mean by 'human' values? It is easy enough, in a land where more real Christianity has been practised than is sometimes supposed, to believe that it is truly 'human' to be kind, just, faithful, unselfish and tolerant. But does the British humanist seriously imagine that such ideas are universally held? Is he really so naïve as to think that they are widely held in, for instance, a Communist-controlled country? And if not, who is to say what is really 'human'? Where are the real standards of right and wrong? It is worth noting in this connection that conference and negotiation between a traditionally Christian country and a Communist country invariably break down because the values held by the parties concerned are not the same. What appears to us to be insincere, false, callous and cruel may be perfectly 'moral' and 'human' by the standards of Communism. It is monstrous to suggest that whole races of people have suddenly ceased to be 'human'! But it is perfectly possible that they have conformed to a view of life which is quite antipathetic to the one which we traditionally hold. Yet if we say that they have been 'deceived' or are 'mistaken' or have been indoctrinated by 'false' ideas then we are passing moral judgments, and the moment we do that we are implying that there *are* standards of good and evil. Without some knowledge of pattern and purpose behind life, what constitutes 'a good human being' can vary so enormously as to make any definition nonsensical.

Humanism denies men any religion, any supra-human standard, any timeless point of reference; and without any of these things I do not believe humanists have a leg to stand on, and it is high time the absurdity of their position were realised. The most a thoroughgoing humanist can do is to express his own opinion about what is 'good' and 'right', and there may be a hundred different views about that! And I cannot help commenting that the very same intellectual humanists whom I have met, and who can speak so convincingly about the uselessness of religion and the sufficiency of scientific humanism, are among those who are quick to point out that 'right' and 'wrong' are purely relative and vary both from country to country and from age to age!

But there are other weaknesses in the atheistic humanist position and they are much more serious than illogicality. Since in the humanist view a man's life is entirely restricted to his consciousness of living on this planet, and since God is totally denied, a conscientious humanist renders himself impotent in many crucial situations. Thus, since there is no life beyond this one, humanism can offer no hope to those who are severely handicapped. Since there is no God, it can offer no external power to guide and strengthen a man who is defeated by his own emotional conflicts. Humanists are themselves prisoners of a closed-system and, since they believe in it so tenaciously, they have no gospel of any kind to offer to the weak and struggling, and can offer neither hope nor security beyond the ills and accidents of this present stage of existence.

Sometimes I cannot help suspecting that some of the atheistic humanists who write and talk so brilliantly have had very little experience of life 'in the raw'. For I know, as many others know, that in the crises of life men and women not only reach out desperately for God but quite often find him. You cannot visit hospital wards, for example, week after week for many years, you cannot attend many deathbeds and speak with literally thousands of bereaved people over the years without realising what potentialities there are in the spirit of apparently quite ordinary people. Personal contact with many suffering, loving and sorrowing people convinces one that man does not live only in this dimension of time, and that no amount of humanist docketing will confine him to it. It is not merely that human beings in their hour of need show tremendous courage, although this is true. Quite ordinary people reach out and touch powers beyond themselves and use them. They receive solid assurance that goes far beyond their tentative hopes. Those of us who have had much to do with the sick and suffering know how common it is for people to tell us that they have drawn upon reserves outside themselves or rested their hopes and fears upon a serenity apparently quite independent of their own minds. Most of them describe this in religious terms, rightly, as I believe, but even if it were not so described I cannot doubt that it is part of the total human picture. I have used the example of human behaviour in pain and suffering because it is under those conditions that insincerity, pretence and habitual self-deception are most easily stripped off.

I know perfectly well that the militant humanist will tell me that I am merely describing subjective phenomena. But the whole point is that what I have observed results in objective phenomena – courage, faith, hope, joy and patience, for instance, and these qualities are very readily observed. For while the kind-hearted humanist can at the very most only rally a man's own resources, the one who has some experience of a power outside himself can invite others to share it with him. This will mean fulfilling certain conditions, and if the result were merely a subjective experience it would scarcely be worthwhile. But if it results in a new sort of reality being apprehended, the effects of which are objective and demonstrable in terms of human living, then surely it is very valuable indeed.

The man who wants everything proved by scientific means is quite right in his insistence on 'laboratory conditions' if he is investigating, shall we say, water-divining, clairvoyance or telekinesis. But there can be no such thing as 'laboratory conditions' for investigating the realm of the human spirit unless it can be seen that the 'laboratory conditions' are in fact human life itself. A man can only exhibit objectively a change in his own disposition, a faith which directs his life and a belief in its significance, *in the actual business of living*. And this is precisely where I join issue with the humanist. If I had not seen objective results springing from faith in spiritual realities, I should no more believe in God than the most thoroughgoing atheist.

But what really puzzles me is the attitude of mind adopted by the humanist who denies the existence of God. He claims that his own life has a purpose, and that other people's lives have their various purposes, but he emphatically denies that there is any purpose in the whole. Moreover, since he also denies any further existence beyond that of this planet, there can be no sense whatever of ultimate purpose of any kind. For the whole tale of man's struggles, discoveries, achievements, insights and aspirations ends automatically when this little planet becomes either too hot or too cold to support human life. I honestly find it impossible to believe that men who are otherwise quite intelligent can seriously think, as they appear to do, that the end of the whole vast human experiment is sheer nothingness. I think I can understand a man willingly devoting his life to posterity, even if he is unable to believe in his own personal survival of death. But what I cannot believe is that it is worth anybody's while to give time, talents and energy to something that finally is utterly without worth.

Now I am well aware that one of our modern humanists might interrupt at this stage and say, 'Now your religion, your belief in God and immortality are put up by your mind, simply because it will not face the true facts – the utter loneliness and futility of human living.' But, quite apart from other arguments, which I will advance later, I am perfectly entitled to retort, 'But suppose *your* attitude is also one of wishful thinking! It is because you cannot bear to believe you are set on this temporary stage to develop responsible moral character, and because you cannot tolerate the idea that this is only the first of what may be many stages of conscious existence that you deny completely the idea of God and of life on any other plane but the terrestrial. You are deliberately lopping off certain human experiences because they do not fit in with your theory of closed-system humanism.'

I am convinced that there is a true humanism, which flows not from a vague Christian tradition but from a quickened sense of the meaning and purpose of God. I am further convinced that the true love of mankind springs more readily and more potently from the Christian faith than from any other religion. Such a love of humanity is no enemy of science or knowledge, but it can add a quality and a depth to living which are impossible without a true religious faith. The particular brand of scientific humanism which affects so much of our thinking is either agnostic, in the less narrow sense of that term, or rigidly atheistic. And a system which denies the existence of God, the possibility of touching extra-human spiritual resources, and any dimension of human living except that which is lived upon this planet, seems to me to be a pathetically inadequate philosophy for the complex spirit of man.

Chapter Five

THE LIMITATIONS OF SCIENCE

Let us be clear in our minds that there is a sharp difference between the attitude of the dedicated man of science and the man who, with little real knowledge of science, sees in it the answer to all the problems of humanity. The truly great scientist, as far as my experience and reading inform me, is a humble man. He unravels one complexity only to discover that the small door which he has opened reveals vista after vista of further complexities. He can hardly escape an over-whelming sense of awe. It is true that he may find himself unable to accept those childish conceptions of 'God' which are all that perhaps have come his way, but frequently he is a deeply religious man. He knows how little he knows, and that is for all of us the beginning of wisdom. But that attitude of mind is poles apart from that of the man who thinks only in terms of the revolutionary contributions which science has made to human living on the material plane. Such a man thinks that the answers to all questions will inevitably be produced by scientific knowledge. To him, all that art or religion or philosophy have to say is really quite beside the point; science will lead him by sure and certain methods to heaven upon earth. I am not suggesting that many people would consciously express such a blind and arrogant view of life, but I am concerned to point out that it exists beneath the conscious level in a great many people's minds. We need to see clearly how 'scientism' has become a kind of sacred cow. Its infallibility is often accepted without question, and its limitations lie unsuspected. In Dr Magnus Pyke's book,

Nothing Like Science,[1] we have a most significant sidelight on the sanctity of this modern god. For the author states in one place that he once proposed to give a broadcast talk on 'The Failures of Science'. *He was not allowed to do so* – apparently because to debunk what is held by many to be infallible would be the ultimate heresy!

Let us take some simple illustrations of the limitations of science. By the use of scientific methods we can be told accurately and completely about the sound produced in the playing of a Beethoven sonata or a Bach fugue. There is not the slightest deviation in tempo or pitch, not the smallest variation in harmonic or overtone which is not readily measurable by the appropriate instruments. But by such analysis would any sane person consider that science had done anything whatever to *explain* the music, to give the slightest clue to its effect upon human emotional experience, still less to explain why one piece of music should be great and the other mediocre? Similarly, in the art of painting, science may give the most complete physical and chemical analysis of a certain canvas, but can do absolutely nothing to explain its value or its effect. Thus science by its very nature and method is excellently equipped for dealing with physical matters, whether the problems arise in the conquest of disease, the fatigue of metals or corrosion by sea water – to name but three which come to mind – but by the very same token science is quite irrelevant in the field of any of the arts, or of philosophy or of religion. There are realms of human experience where the scientific method, as commonly understood, is simply not the right instrument to use. Indeed it would be as inappropriate to attempt scientific analysis in some human situations as it would be to use a microphone to detect odour, or a geiger-counter to measure the consumption of domestic gas! In the nature of the complex human situation of which we are a part it must be understood that there are aspects and dimensions of truth which are vital to man's well-being

[1] John Murray.

on which science has nothing to say. Because science can answer so many of our *hows* we should not be deceived into thinking that it can answer any of our *whys*.

Of course we all owe an incalculable debt to the science which is applied to our common life. I confess I have no patience at all with those who long to return to some fanciful pre-scientific age. Who would wish to go back to an age in which there was no electricity for lighting, heating or power, no printed books, no piped water, no roads, no charted seas, no reliable means of communication, no anaesthetics, no antibiotics or sulpha-drugs, no real understanding of physical or mental illness – in fact to lapse back into ignorance? But at the same time my commonsense and my experience tell me that many of the really intransigent problems in human life are hardly touched at all by such scientific advances.

There seems to me to be a danger for some lest they become drunk with scientific achievement and imagine that if only men make bigger and better technical strides then all 'human' problems will solve themselves. Again, this is not an error into which any of us would fall consciously, but I believe it lurks dangerously in many unconscious minds. Surely it is not unreasonable to plead that more of the admirable patience and dedication required for scientific advance should be directed upon really pressing human needs. Is it not a measure of our bewitchment by science that modern man should be seriously planning to visit another planet within measurable time when there are a thousand unsolved economic, social and moral problems on his own? We can think at once of the problem of 'integration' with people whose skins are variously pigmented, of the problems of nations emerging from centuries of primitive ignorance, of the problem of health and nutrition of millions of people in 'the East'. We can think of the problem of cancer or of poliomyelitis, of the increasing number of people who are mentally sick, of the thousands of broken homes, of the juvenile delinquent, and of the special problems of the blind, the deaf, the dumb, the spastic and of the mentally defective. These are but a few of the dozens of urgent human problems which surely challenge man's enterprise, compassion and willingness to serve. Yet, in actual fact, there is a tragic dearth of people willing to dedicate their lives to coping with them. Is not this also an indication of the extent to which man has become intoxicated by a false idea of science?

We have already reached the point where the discoveries of science can 'greatly bless or wholly destroy'. But the way in which the knowledge is used cannot be decided by scientific means. The majority of scientific men are without doubt kindly and humane people, but it is not their science which gives them their kindness or their humanity, nor can any branch of science assess what is 'good' or 'right' or 'human'. Science itself is incapable of making moral judgments, and it is not really too wild a step of the imagination to think of a situation where scientific knowledge is valued more highly than human lives. In countries where our traditional 'Christian' values are not held it seems to me perfectly possible that science could become the master instead of the servant.

Most of the activities of what is commonly called science are concerned with the physical and the material. But there are departments of scientific knowledge which do touch what I believe is our crucial problem, the problem of human behaviour. The comparatively newly-born science of psychology can offer much illumination and disentanglement. Enormous loads of human unhappiness have been lifted by wise and patient psychiatrists. Men and women have been reintegrated into society, human relationships have been vastly improved and a host of hitherto insoluble problems have been successfully dealt with by skilled psychological methods.

The curing of mental ill-health, enabling an individual to fit happily into normal social life, demands great patience and skill. We cannot be other than full of gratitude and admiration for those who devote their lives to such demanding work. But we might properly ask whether such adjustment, valuable as it is to the community as it exists, is sufficient. It may be doing no more than producing a well-shaped cog instead of an ill-shaped cog for use, for instance, in industrial life; it cannot integrate a man into the total pattern and purpose for human living, and does not attempt to do so. It is well known that the man-hours lost to industry through mental sickness of one kind or another reach an alarming figure. We may be sure that a Communist country is as quick as we are to use psychiatric methods to cure such mental sickness, if only in order to maintain the efficiency of its factory personnel. But such treatment would inevitably leave the godless, Communist-indoctrinated attitude of the patients as it was before. The Communist psychiatrist, or our Western psychiatrist has, we will say, performed his work skilfully and well. He has helped the patient to 'adjust himself to life', but in either case he has helped a human being to fit into a pattern of human life without giving him any clue as to whether it is the right pattern.

We gratefully acknowledge that psychiatry can, and does, remove certain disabilities and resolve certain conflicts, but it cannot by itself supply our standards or values. It cannot answer any questions outside the immediate range of human personality. I believe that those who would see in modern psychiatry something at once more efficient and more 'scientific' than true religion are doomed to disappointment. For however excellent psychiatric methods may be, no adjustment can be provided towards any supra-human purpose in life and no connection made with any resource outside human personality. Such further integration may be, and of course sometimes is, provided, even unconsciously, by the psychiatrist. But that is because he is a man of faith himself, and not because he is a practitioner in psychiatry. He has to go beyond his function as a scientist if he is to adjust his patient to a world of spiritual reality.

Obviously this whole business of 'adjustment to life' raises fundamental questions. Unless we have some standards beyond the immediate human situation, the most we can do is to help fit a man into the existing social fabric.

But suppose that our whole social fabric is wrong, then our good, well-adjusted man is only good and well-adjusted in our opinion, in a certain context and under certain conditions. This is, of course, the cue for the humanist to appear and advocate his 'human' values. But let me repeat that the man who denies the existence of God or any spiritual order can only produce a set of ethical standards which he and his friends have decided are the best and most conducive to human happiness. He can have no sort of answer for the millions of people who sharply disagree with his concepts, and who is to say who is right?

Now I know from conversations which I have had with scientists that their whole method of training and pattern of working makes it difficult for them to conceive the apprehension of valid truth by any 'non-scientific' methods. This, by an effort of the imagination, I think I can begin to understand. But I would appeal to any scientist who happens to be reading this book to think seriously that people such as poets, artists of every kind, mystics and indeed ordinary people of faith may be receiving truth in an entirely different way from that to which he is accustomed. It is not in the least that his own wholly admirable and painstaking methods are being ignored or, so to speak, short-circuited. It is simply that there are ways of apprehending some kinds of truth which are quite independent of the scientific method. Sometimes these are intuitive and sometimes they are developed by long practice, and of course sometimes they are both. I think the honest scientist cannot help admitting this, and perhaps he may be persuaded to see what I myself find quite plain – that the more man's attention is concentrated upon the material the more his spiritual faculties become atrophied. I hope he will be good-humoured enough to realise that such a chapter as I have just written is not meant to be an attack upon science but an attack upon that one-sided obsession with the material and the tangible which leads to the loss of spiritual apprehension. Man cannot live in any real sense by science alone.

Chapter Six

THE BEGINNING OF WISDOM

I believe I am right in saying that no primitive race or tribe has ever been discovered without a religion of some sort. Of course it can easily be argued that since primitive man is far more vulnerable than we are he has to invent, out of his fear and insecurity, 'gods' with greater knowledge and power than he has himself. We may further argue that primitive people have to invent 'sanctions' or 'taboos' for the regulation of tribal life. There must be some authority commonly agreed upon which transcends the wishes and powers of any individual. Further, we cannot leave out of our consideration the action of the human conscience, however variable and misguided it may sometimes be. A sense of guilt and fear is found in most primitive peoples and that inevitably leads to rites of propitiation and sacrifice. Life is both mysterious, and awe-inspiring and death, in its starkness and finality, is always at the elbow of primitive man. In some way, simple or complicated, horrible or beautiful, he has to reassure himself that the death of the body is not the death of the human spirit.

Now at a superficial glance all primitive religions are no more than a natural defence-mechanism against man's ignorance, fear and insecurity. Consequently if these last three were reduced we should expect to find the decay of 'religion'. To some extent of course we have seen this happen, although it would be a bold man indeed who would claim that today's 'civilised' world was free from ignorance, fear and insecurity! Nevertheless, as mysteries of the natural world are 'explained', and as man gains more and more mastery over Nature, one particular necessity to invent 'gods' tends to die away. That side of nearly all religion which is produced by fear, ignorance and superstition will obviously be dissolved in the light of scientific knowledge. And that is all to the good. But for myself I would consider it quite unwarrantable to assume that the need for religion has been abolished. A primitive religion may express itself in very primitive ways indeed, but when we come to examine its heart and essence we find it to be far more than a defence against fear and ignorance. It contains in it, in however crude a form, basic human longings, which I do not believe we have in any sense outgrown. There is a desire to discover supernatural laws for human happiness, a willingness to co-operate with a purpose higher than the transitory human purpose, a longing to communicate with the Creator and an attempt to grasp some security which transcends physical death.

Civilised man is insulated far more than he realises from the raw material of living. Most of the exchange of intelligent ideas today takes place, I believe, under strongly protected conditions. Man's sense of wonder is blunted by many inventions, his solitariness upon the planet is concealed from him by the presence of many people, and the highly competitive world in which he makes his living stifles any lingering yearning for anything outside it. However expert he may be in his own particular field, his actual experience of life is far smaller than he realises. Ideas and emotions are often not stimulated by life itself, but by the mediated experience of other people. The newspapers, radio, television, the cinema and the theatre all create in him an illusion of experience. His first-hand knowledge of human living is usually restricted to a small circle of intimate friends, and between them they have worked out a more or less reasonable code of conduct for their department of life. It is hardly surprising that the modern urban worker rarely sees any need for any kind of religion. Obviously we cannot undo the process of 'civilisation' which has made us what we are, but at least we can make some attempt to see how it cushions and blinkers us.

At this point, then, I would put in a strong plea for a more realistic grasp of our human position, for more true humility. Whether our view of life be 'scientific' or 'religious' or both, it would seem only sane and proper for man to feel a sense of awe. He is but a part, and in all probability an extremely small part, of this astonishing universe. The sensitive thinking man is probably aware of this, but he may be quite unaware that for vast numbers of people the capacity for awe, wonder and humility has been exhausted or numbed by the bewildering advance of modern knowledge. Human beings have scarcely caught their breath after one achievement before they are confronted with yet another. They have no time to assess the worth of what has been accomplished, still less to value it in relation to the total human situation. This is surely where the thinkers and writers must come in and make some attempt to restore the balance.

I believe that it is necessary for us to recover a certain salutary humility before we can discern pattern and purpose in our present stage of human existence. I do not in the least mean that we should disregard scientific knowledge or that we should somehow restrict or distrust it, but simply that we should realise our own inherent limitations. We have to accept that our status and our standpoint in the totality of creation are both lowly and circumscribed. For example, astronomers are constantly telling us how foolish, indeed how arrogant, it is to regard the planet on which we live as in any sense the centre of the universe around us. But in condemning the arrogance of such geocentric thinking we should beware of another, subtler arrogance – that of supposing that the sum total of truth can be gathered, sorted and interpreted on this earth where we live! We are quite literally in no position to ascertain all the facts, and what monstrous conceit makes any man suppose that, if we had them, we have the intelligence and the wisdom to understand them? Astronomy itself provides a telling parable of our limitations. The development of the radio telescope alone, with a range thousands of times greater than that of the optical telescope, can give us information of certain happenings in the universe millions of light-years away. We are naturally enormously impressed by this reaching out into space, but our wonder can easily blind us to the fact that astronomy is always telling us of *what has happened in the past*. It can only say that such-and-such an event took place almost countless millions of years ago. It has absolutely no means of judging what is happening *now*. It can, for instance, tell us that the universe is expanding very rapidly. What it really amounts to is that we know beyond reasonable doubt that the universe *was* expanding a very long time ago. We cannot know what is happening now, at this point of earth-time, and indeed for all we know the universe may be rapidly contracting! Now there is no cure whatever for this kind of limitation, and it seems to me but one instance of the intrinsic limit of the human situation, and this might reasonably be expected to recur in other fields in man's search for truth.

I do not think we need be either depressed or surprised at this, but I do think we must learn to live with it as one of the facts of our existence. It often seems to me when listening to the talk of clever people that they are in effect saying, 'Unless I understand, unless I am let into all the secrets of the Creator, I shall refuse to believe in him at all.' I am sure that such an attitude, even if it be unconscious, creates a strong barrier between man and his understanding of his true position.

Anyone with the most elementary knowledge of physics knows that there are sounds which are too high in pitch for us to hear, and forms of light which are quite invisible to the human eye. Nowadays we accept as commonplace the fact that we can devise instruments which can 'hear' and 'see' for us. Yet for some curious reason we find it very difficult to believe that there may be sense higher than our sense, reason above our reason, and a total purpose quite beyond our comprehension. It seems to me perfectly possible that there may be supra-human wisdom, and we might well assume an attitude of wholesome humility when we reflect upon our relative insignificance. Can we not accept the suggestion that there are facts, even 'scientific' facts, which we can never know because we are incapable of understanding them? Can we not be persuaded to believe that specks of consciousness on this little planet cannot, in all reasonableness, be thought of as accurate critics of the total purpose behind creation? I believe it to be essential for us to appreciate our inescapable limitations before the results of our observations and experience can make any sense to us. We do have to become as little children – which is in fact what we are, comparatively – before we can begin to appreciate anything of the plan or purpose of the Creator.

I make no plea for obscurantism or 'blind faith', but rather that men and women should find their proper place in the universe. This is precisely where a real religion, which takes proper account of human limitations and of the Creative Mind which knows no limitations, can provide sense and sanity in our bewilderment.

Chapter Seven

THE NECESSITY FOR TRUE RELIGION

I believe a recovery of real religion to be essential to the well-being of modern humanity. But, alas, the very word 'religion' has the wrong associations for many. They think of Puritanism, of churchiness, of spiritual restriction, of taboos, of dreary church services and sentimental hymns, of pious legend, of traditional thinking, of the attempt to squeeze all truth into a narrow religious mould, of the inefficiency and blindness of some churches, of the hypocrites who profess one thing and obviously believe another, of blind faith with its fear of true knowledge, of the pride of those who believe that they alone hold the truth – and so on, *ad nauseam*. And yet what I am pleading for when I urge a return to real religion is something quite different. It must mean a willing adjustment to our situation as human beings in the whole creation, and that must mean accepting a relationship not only with other human beings but with the Spirit behind the whole scheme. As I have said above, we are children living largely in the dark, but we are not wholly without clues. We have reason, we have critical faculties, we have a more-or-less developed moral sense, we have intuitions and intimations which point to something beyond the here-and-now. We have, too, enough accumulated human experience to show what patterns of human conduct lead to misery and disaster, and what can lead to happiness and fulfilment.

The humanists would say that we have enough without supernatural religion – with all our knowledge and experience there is surely no need to postulate a spiritual world and a supreme being called God. It would be pleasant to believe that they are right as far as they go, and that a little spiritual superstructure is all that is needed to turn a humanist into a truly religious man. But my experience and observation convince me more and more that the humanist position is quite unrealistic. For one thing it never takes serious account of evil. In humanist thinking the reason why people behave badly, cruelly or selfishly can always be explained in economic, political or psychological terms. Human perversity, callousness and brutality, when exhibited in sufficient quantity, lead the humanist mind to the end of its tether. Yet, to be frank, it has no remedy to offer except good advice!

It is all very well to be a humanist and exhibit 'human' values if you are a reasonably well-adjusted, kindly, tolerant, honest and decent person. In all probability you habitually exert a certain amount of self-discipline of your own thoughts and feelings, and probably you do not see why others cannot readily do the same. But suppose your temperament is a mass of contradictions and that you find it extremely difficult to be kindly and tolerant. Suppose that by nature you have no great interest outside yourself and have no desire to serve other people or ameliorate their lot. Suppose that you are only too aware of evil in yourself which vitiates relationships and dries up the springs of compassion. Is there, then, no hope for you to be a good human being?

This is to me the very heart of the whole matter. If there is no restoring force, no healing and rehabilitating Spirit, no extra-human source of goodness and compassion, then many of us are undone indeed. If I did not know that there was such restoration and reinforcement, that there are such springs which can be tapped by human beings, I should naturally not be writing this book at all. But here is a field of actual human experience, disgracefully neglected and very imperfectly explored, which could make a radical change in our human condition. It is a fine thing to say that unless we learn to exercise more love and compassion for one another we shall end up by destroying one another. But unless we can implement that rhetoric by exploring a power wiser and greater than mere humanity we are doing no more than underlining the obvious. For the more we examine the human situation – and the more we can do of this at first-hand the better – the more we see that a deficiency of love is the root-cause of nearly all our most refractory problems. Juvenile delinquency, for example, may be traced back to a childhood starved of love, and juvenile delinquency is never cured without the wise application of love. Marriages break up because love diminishes. Industrial relationships become embittered, men and women are cheated, exploited and deceived simply because there is a lack of love. It is time the very word 'love' was rehabilitated, for probably no other single word has been so grossly misused. But the true love of which the world stands in such desperate need is compassionate and wise, strong and patient. Wisdom, cleverness, experience and psychological 'know-how' are all useful tools in dealing with human situations, but unless they are used by love no situation is permanently changed and no human attitude radically altered. That is a matter of observable experience.

But to adopt the way of informed, constructive love is necessarily costly to the personality. And nowhere do we see more clearly the terrible lack of real love than in the scarcity of people willing to give themselves in coping with dark, difficult and messy situations. Why is there a chronic shortage of nurses and midwives? Why such a lack of those willing to nurse the mentally ill, or care for the physically handicapped? Why indeed is there such a lamentable shortage of leaders for youth organisations, of prison-visitors, of doctors willing to go to the disease-ridden parts of the world? Why are there so few volunteers in the really needy centres of human misery – why are there so few whose love extends any further than their own circle? Why are works of human compassion nearly always left to be operated by a mere handful on a shoestring budget? Why indeed, unless there is a tragic and worldwide deficiency of outgoing love?

Unless we are totally blind to human situations as they really exist, we cannot avoid the conclusion that without a revolutionary quality of living the human race is doomed to an endless process of unproductive suffering or even of total extinction. Even if a few should survive a nuclear world war there is absolutely no guarantee that the same dangerous situations would not reappear. Much as we may dislike the doctrine of original sin – and indeed it has often been formulated in a way that must antagonise any man of sense and goodwill – there would appear to be in human beings the seeds of selfishness, arrogance, brutality, callousness, the lust for power, jealousy, hatred and all the rest of the miserable host of evil. I do not believe that we serve the cause of truth or of humanity if we insist that these things have no real existence, when in fact they may be merely dormant or unprovoked. A realistic view of human life demands that we take into account the evil as well as the good in human nature.

To me it seems perfectly plain that there can be no satisfactory human living, feeling and thinking without a true religion. For example, men can without much difficulty regard one another as comrades and brothers in undertaking some difficult enterprise provided that their basic ideals are more or less the same. Those who are opposed to the ideals of such a band of comrades must be either converted or destroyed. Without true religion I cannot see anything illogical in this process. The intrinsic value of the individual, his dignity and his freedom only become meaningful to us when we see him standing in the same relationship to the Creator as we do ourselves. Without recognition of the Creator, without some apprehension of a good over-all purpose for all human beings in whatever stage of development they may be, to consider all other men as our brothers is no more than a pious phrase. And certainly, without access to resources of patience and compassion beyond one's normal human endowment, most of us would have to face life with no more than a stoic despair.

If this little precarious foothold upon earth is all that we are ever to know of conscious living, if in fact there is no life except the material and physical, those of us who are not particularly altruistic by nature would hardly think our labours and struggles worthwhile. Why should we not eat, drink and be merry? For tomorrow we die. But suppose this is not true. There are many besides myself who know that when we allow ourselves to be used by a purpose much greater than we are, we become conscious of fitting into a pattern with a feeling of permanence, a pattern only incompletely outlined in the here-and-now. If this be true, as many of us are convinced it is, then life itself, ourselves, our neighbours and all the crying needs of the world take on a new significance. This little life with its incurable limitations, its apparent injustices and pointless tragedies, its hopes, disappointments and frustrations, is seen as no more than the outcrop in time-and-space of a vast process which we can only begin to discern.

But such a view of life, which at once accepts man's present limitations and believes in his ultimate potentialities, is only possible to the one who has true religious faith. The man who has no religion, and denies the possibility of there being any such thing, imprisons himself within the closed-system of physical life upon this planet. This is the position of the agnostic who, according to the Oxford dictionary definition is '*one who holds that nothing is known, or likely to be known of the existence of a God or of anything beyond material phenomena*'. The dreams of the poet, the visions of the artist, the 'pattern' apprehended by the truly religious man, have all to be explained as purely subjective phenomena within the material set-up. All the hopes, joys, inklings and intuitions which seem to have a point of reference outside the physical world must be shown up for the illusion that they are. Every 'intimation of immortality', every 'sunset touch', every sense of awe and wonder and mystery have to be seen through and explained away. For the true agnostic the material dimension is the only dimension. There is no reality beyond this reality, no purpose and no God.

Yet I would doubt very much whether the majority of those who call themselves 'agnostics' would accept the dictionary definition. They are much more like people who 'don't know' than like those who would definitely assert that no one can ever know anything at all in fields beyond the material. False religion, prejudiced and perverted religion, arrogant and self-opinionated religion have unhappily made them distrust the religious approach to truth. Yet I say with some knowledge that there are modern agnostics who have never given ten minutes' serious adult critical study to what real religion stands for. They have allowed themselves to be put off by the hypocrites, the obscurantists and the lovers of power, who exist in any religious system – as they do elsewhere. I am concerned here to plead that such people should examine the religious approach *de novo*, and be prepared to give such a widespread human phenomenon as religion their serious attention. The man who possesses a strong religious faith knows very well that there are hundreds of questions which are likely to remain unanswered, at any rate in this life. But he is in possession of a strong clue to reality and a conviction that he is co-operating with a purpose transcending present observed material phenomena.

Chapter Eight

RELIGION AND MODERN KNOWLEDGE

The heart of all real religions is an affirmation that human life on this planet is only part of something very much greater; that 'human values' are determined by an authority higher than human beings themselves; and that man neither finds happiness nor discovers his true self until his worship, his loyalty and his love are given to Someone infinitely greater than any person or group. Through the great religions of the world man is trying to find some clue to the mystery of life and to find some expression of those longings within himself which transcend the confines of ordinary material existence. In short, however crude his attempts, he is trying to prove that he is more than a physical entity. It appears inevitable that with the passage of the centuries the world's great religions are inclined to become complicated and corrupted. Even in the best cases it may be difficult for the modern observer to penetrate to the original intention of the founder of a religion, while in the worst cases the pristine spirit has been entirely suffocated. It is therefore essential for the modern person who attempts to understand religious truth to get behind the accretions, distortions and degenerations and try to see the original light.

As modern knowledge advances and hitherto insoluble problems are solved, a good deal of religion will be seen to be based on false premises, to be inadequate for modern conceptions of the universe, or to be little more than a collection of superstitious taboos. In our day whole nations who have been held in fear and ignorance by certain religious systems are being released almost overnight, as it were, by the rising tide of modern knowledge. This is happening in the continents of Asia and Africa, for example, and insofar as people are being set free from ignorance, superstition and fear we cannot but be glad. But that is not the whole story. For if nothing is put in the place of the old religion then they are left with a greatly diminished sense of their own value. With the old taboos gone and the authority of the old gods exploded, moral standards are the first casualties. Under the old religion a person had status, significance and purpose, but with the old beliefs discredited beyond recall, all this very quickly becomes lost and a person sinks into being a mere unit in the mass-mind. This was of course the golden opportunity for Communism. In place of the old vague, 'spiritual' purpose a definite observable programme was set down in concrete terms. Man's place and worth are established, and provided he can disregard any immortal longings he can fit happily into such a comprehensive system. The State takes over the 'father-figure' of God, and the State provides for his needs much more reliably than any of his old capricious gods.

The State makes laws which are plainly for the good of all, and the whole scheme obviously makes more physical and technical progress in a few years than was previously made in as many centuries. We really cannot be surprised that when old religions were shattered Communism moved in and met men's apparent needs. Let us remember that all religions are attempting to say something about man's place in the universe, and are to some extent satisfying his immortal yearnings. The old gods, the old superstitions, the old wives' tales, the fables and the legends have been destroyed, but I see no valid reason why there should not be a recovery of true religion of the kind at which I have hinted above. Moreover, we should be foolish to ignore the significance of any religion, however faulty and inadequate. Let me illustrate what I mean. As modern medicine advances throughout the world the superstitions and mumbo-jumbo of magic-medicine very naturally disappear. But even in the most ignorant and primitive medicine there existed the desire to heal, and that desire has not been superseded. Thus it seems to me that although the acids of modern thought may quickly dissolve myth and superstition, nothing can destroy the basic need which led to the emergence of religion. A false view of 'the gods' may easily be blown away by the first breath of scientific knowledge, but a true faith in God is not destroyed but rather enhanced by every fresh discovery of the complexity of God's wisdom. I believe the time may come when it will seem ludicrous for men to discover layer after layer of truth which bear all the marks of pattern and design, and then categorically to declare that there is no Designer! I see nothing far-fetched in the idea that man may one day consider it just as important to make spiritual discoveries and live in harmony with the spiritual pattern as he now thinks it important to discover, and co-operate with, physical laws.

It has sometimes been suggested that what modern man needs is a religion composed of all the best elements of the existing world religions, purged of course of their magical, superstitious and miraculous elements and presented in an ethical form which might win widespread acceptance among men of goodwill. It could be argued that such a synthetic religion would provide a suitable acknowledgment of the Supreme Wisdom behind all observable phenomena, and while properly respecting the visions and ideals of religious founders, would not affront modern intelligence by retaining what is plainly irrational. It is only when we come to examine the world's religions in some detail that we realise the impossibility of such a synthesis. Naturally, in all religions there is a common denominator of human ethics, although even this is not as high as some humanists with a Christian tradition behind them would suppose. It is when we come to study the basic conceptions of God, the relationship between man and God, the impact of belief upon social conduct and the view of life after death, that we realise how wide and deep is the gulf between the leading religions. If we attempt to combine them into one modern super-religion we are left with something very like humanism. For since human beings would be the judges of which tenets are included and which are excluded we find ourselves back again in the closed humanist world which denies supernatural revelation. Thus I believe it is essential to have revelation if we are to have a religion which can give purpose and power to human living. To my mind there must be a breaking through into human life of information about an order both supra-human and ultra-human. Otherwise the best we can do is to form an ethical society with its objectives and horizon limited to this planet.

It is not my purpose, and indeed it is not within my competence, to write a book about Comparative Religion. There are several such books quite readily available for those who want to study the subject. But I must make a few observations to underline the impossibility of synthesising the great religions. For example, according to Islam, God is a strict unity and although compassionate he is predominantly a God of power rather than of love. God and man are permanently separate; God orders man's destiny (Kismet) and freedom is an illusion. Sin is as much foreordained as righteousness. Conversion may be forcible, and women are regarded as inferior to men. Of course many Muslims are better than their creed, but we can at once see how irreconcilable Islam is, for example, with Christianity. The central point of the Christian Faith is the indissoluble link between God and man, expressed through Christ; man is free to choose either good or evil; God's purpose is to bring all people into the right relationship with himself; and in the teaching of Christ there is neither class distinction, colour bar, nor discrimination between the sexes. In fact the only common ground between Christianity and Islam is the belief that God is infinitely greater than man and is a God to be worshipped and served. Now what compatibility can we find between these two great faiths, and either Buddhism or Hinduism, in which millions have their only experience of religion? Again, to pick a few random but important points

– Buddha himself was agnostic about the existence of God. He held that the question had no bearing on practical living. Consequently any problems of the relationship between God and man simply do not arise. Sin, which is a matter of anti-social behaviour, results in repeated unpleasant reincarnations into this present world, while the ultimate state is the abolition of either existence or desire (Nirvana). Now although the teaching of Buddha contains much that is beautiful and compassionate, it is a known fact that in predominantly Buddhist countries for centuries very little was done to relieve suffering or ameliorate the lot of other people. After all, if a man were working out atonement for sins in a past life by his present suffering, what right had anyone to interfere with the process? Hinduism is also equally difficult to combine with any other world religion. Within it are enormous varieties of philosophical and popular belief. Common ground with Buddhism may be found in the doctrines of rebirth and Nirvana, but there are many contradictory notions held within the framework of this religious system. It has been observed with some truth that, at any rate in the past, a Hindu could believe anything so long as he observed caste, reverenced the cow and accepted the Veda as revelation! According to Hindu philosophy God is the unknowable Absolute, while at the same time man *is* God, the apparent distinction being due to illusion (maya), which in turn is due to ignorance (avidya). Within the almost unbelievable latitude of belief allowed by Hinduism there stands out the most rigid caste system which the world has ever known. Of course it is true that this system is being slowly broken down under the various modern pressures, but it remains an essential part of official Hinduism, and a lasting memorial to man's religious inhumanity to man.

Let us think of another great world religion, Judaism, the religion of the Jews. It is indeed hard not to be thought unfair to this monotheistic religion which has given so much to the moral thinking of the Western world. A religion which could produce the Ten Commandments and the inspired writing of the Old Testament prophets, for example, cannot but command the greatest respect, while those of us who are Christians should never forget that the teaching of the New Testament sprang historically from Judaism. It is only when we come to examine the religion of the Jews more closely that we find its severe limitations. It tends to be both backward-looking and inward-looking and it is a religion for one people only, containing no intention of embracing the whole of mankind within its system. Orthodox Judaism by its very nature cannot be combined with or incorporated into any other religious creed. It can never become the religion for modern Gentile man.

I should like to make it plain at this point that I am not saying that there do not exist within the great world religions true, honest, wise and good men. Of course there are many such, and many men and women rise far above the spirit of their particular creed. Furthermore, Eastern religions, despite that wealth of fantasy, myth and legend which make them quite unacceptable to modern minds with an historic sense, possess a keen perception of the spiritual as opposed to the material. They underline the virtues of quiet meditation, of contemplation and of control of the body by the mind and spirit in a way which is foreign to most Western minds, but which might yet prove valuable to modern Western man in his busy, noise-infested world. Thus, while we are bound to reject the fictitious and fanciful content of Eastern religions, we might do well to accept techniques of practising religion which we in the West have almost wholly neglected.

But if we are to find a religious system which cannot be outdated or outgrown, from which the acids of modernity can only remove accretions and encrustations, a religion which properly practised produces the highest forms of human behaviour, and offers both supernatural pattern and spiritual power beyond human endeavour, then I believe we shall have to take a fresh look at Christianity. We shall have to look at it with new eyes, forgetting the distortions, suppressions and misapprehensions to which it has been subjected over the centuries. We shall have to overlook men's blindness to its revolutionary character, their stupidity in attempting to confine the spiritual within the temporal and their many sad demonstrable failures in Christian living. Then we may be able to touch again the heart and centre of something which I believe reorientates the whole of human thinking, feeling and action.

Chapter Nine

A NEW LOOK AT CHRISTIANITY

Although the moral standards and ethical judgments of this country have long been permeated by Christian teaching, there is a widespread ignorance both of the actual history of the Christian faith and of its revolutionary character. Generally speaking, there is no intake of Christian information and consequently no attempt to see the relevance of basic Christian principles in modern situations. It is not, I repeat, that the thinkers, the writers, and the leaders of popular thought, in whatever media, have for the most part studied Christianity and rejected it as unhistoric, impractical and outdated. It is simply that they have not studied it at all! I believe their attitude of almost total ignorance to be quite indefensible, and I find myself in agreement with a friend of mine who was to discuss on television the Christian position with four leading London journalists. He asked them simply whether any one of them had given five consecutive minutes (*minutes*, mark you!) to the serious study of what Christianity had to say, and every one of them admitted he had not. Whereupon my friend remarked kindly but firmly that if that were the case no real discussion could possibly take place. In my own experience I find it perfectly extraordinary that men and women of unusual ability in their respective spheres have rarely taken the trouble to give their adult attention to such a unique way of life as that proposed by Jesus Christ. I am happy to admit that there are exceptions, but how often has one met otherwise intelligent people who have dismissed the whole Christian faith because, for instance, they cannot believe that the first chapter of

Genesis is true to science, that Jonah was swallowed by a whale, that unbaptised babies go to hell, or that heaven is above the bright blue sky! Because the Church has been guilty of many glaring faults over the centuries, because Christians have frequently failed to be Christians through cowardice or lethargy, because an archbishop has said a foolish thing, because the methods of some evangelists are not approved, or because of some other quite trivial or irrelevant reason, some people appear to think that Christianity is finally discredited and its challenge can be honourably ignored! Such people are worse than 'touchline critics', for not only are they criticising a game in which they are not themselves involved, but they have never taken the trouble to acquaint themselves with the rules!

If this ignorance is prevalent among the leaders of popular opinion, and I believe it is, we cannot be surprised that most ordinary people have no idea what Christianity is all about. Many of them have no use for the churches, regard clergy and ministers, as a class, with suspicion, but nevertheless have a certain vague respect for the personality of Jesus. The situation is not made any easier by the fact that almost their only source of knowledge of what modern Christians are thinking and doing is their daily newspaper. They therefore get an entirely negative impression; they are apt to read only about such things as a denunciation of gambling or Sunday amusement, a condemnation of modern moral standards, or, now and again, the story of some unhappy parson who has 'gone wrong'. They read nothing in the national Press of what Christianity is all about, and they are given negligible information about either the aims or the work of Christian churches throughout the world. It would therefore hardly be an exaggeration to say that very many people look upon Christianity largely as a repressive system, designed to spoil the pleasures of life and offering a man a rather dubious heaven in some vague world to come. I believe that if it were possible to get people to listen with fresh and unprejudiced minds to what Christianity is really saying, they might not accept it, but at least they could not dismiss it as a hangover from childhood, a beautiful but impractical dream, or as mere 'religion' quite irrelevant to modern living.

Let us for the moment forget all about the churches' reputedly narrow views, their 'dressed-up bishops', their peculiar language and their apparently naïve ignorance of how life has to be lived by millions of people. Let us forget the churches' failures over the centuries and their present disagreements – in fact, let us for the time being forget the churches altogether and get back to the source of the Christian faith. For Christianity begins with an historical fact; indeed its starting-point is the most important event in the whole of human history. The Christian religion asserts that nearly two thousand years ago God, whose vast and complex wisdom science is daily uncovering, visited this small planet of ours in Person. Naturally the only way in which he could do this was by becoming a human being, and this is precisely what Christians believe that he did. This is the heart and centre of the Christian faith, this is the Gospel or Good News which those who had witnessed this extraordinary event went out to tell the then known world. That God so inserted himself into the stream of human history, and that we are consequently living on a visited planet, are statements audacious enough to take the breath away, and no reasonable person could be expected to accept such a belief as fact without considerable thought and careful examination of the evidence. To have had God, reduced in stature to that of a human being, but indubitably God playing a part in the earthly scene, is a staggering thought. But this is where Christianity starts, this is the rock on which it is founded, and this is the point where men are compelled by the nature of the event to make up their minds as to whether it is true or false.

Let us not concern ourselves about how this startling event has been smothered in decoration, blunted by over-familiarity, or overlaid by merely secondary considerations. Nothing must be allowed to distract us from considering with adult minds and hearts whether this is true history or a beautiful myth. The decision is so important that it must not, indeed cannot, be avoided. Yet this is the point at which so many people take evasive action. They begin to hide behind clouds of criticism of the Church or of particular Christians, or they create a diversion by arguing about the historicity of the Old Testament stories, or, for example, about the Church's attitude towards war or divorce. I believe that each one of us must eventually face the real issue, which is quite simply: do I believe after adult examination of the evidence that Jesus Christ was what he claimed to be, or am I prepared to assert quite definitely that he was wrong in his major claims and that, though much of his teaching is beautiful, he himself was a self-deceived fanatic?

Chapter Ten

THE QUESTION OF PROBABILITY

I have sometimes heard people speak of the 'inherent improbability' of the Christian faith, and I must confess that I am never quite sure what they mean. We are not in any real position to assess the 'probability' of anything which happens within the framework of the laws of the universe, and we deceive ourselves if we think we possess an exhaustive knowledge of even these. Many commonplaces of today are the improbabilities of yesterday, and in any branch of science 'improbabilities' occur from time to time which are apparently arbitrary exceptions to previously observed rules. The scientist does not conclude that his observation must therefore be faulty; he notes that the apparent exception is part of the total of observed phenomena. Sometimes he will later discover another law which accounts for what appear to be the exceptions, or he may have to be content for the present to register phenomena as 'exceptional'.

Now we are not living in a lunatic world, but in part of a law-abiding universe, and we are quite right to reject on rational grounds that which outrages reason. We may be perfectly certain, for example, that the Greek goddess Pallas Athene was not born as a fully developed, and fully armed, woman out of the head of her father Zeus! We rightly call that sort of thing myth, and it could never be considered as sober history. But we cannot so dismiss the historic accounts of the birth of Jesus. If we will admit for a moment that God did enter into the human historical process, we may reasonably expect something unusual, something analogous to the 'exceptions' of science. We may have to accept the operation of a law higher than the normal law, but we are not expected to accept an irrational myth. But, of course, the critics of Christianity may mean that the 'improbability' of the faith lies in another direction. We have only to consider how human planning would have arranged such an event, and compare it with what actually happened, to see this kind of improbability! If human planners had been at work no doubt the entry of the Creator into his creation would have been arranged with the maximum of publicity. The family into which he was born would have been the noblest in a nation whose culture represented the peak of human achievement. For his human adventure the Creator would have been provided with the finest clothes, the best books, and surrounded by the most influential friends. The most detailed observation of his life, of all that he said and did, would have been most meticulously kept. No stone would have been left unturned to ensure that everybody knew who this unique person really was. Compared with such a fantasy, the recorded facts are, of course, lamentably 'improbable'. Jesus was born into a family of humble station. His actual birth was in lowly and improvised conditions. His upbringing and education took place in an obscure village with none too good a reputation. His whole career as a preacher and teacher was very limited and sadly cut short, and it all happened in a small, rather despised country occupied by the Roman powers. Of course this appears 'improbable', but may I say in passing that this is the kind of improbability to which we have to become accustomed if we are to have any dealings with the contemporary God. We have to learn to work with a wisdom which follows a pattern quite foreign to much human thinking.

But there is yet another sense in which the Christian story may be thought to be improbable, and that is because it appears to be arbitrarily and even monstrously unjust. If God chooses to reveal himself on this planet in the person of a man, why must whole nations rise and fall before he is even born? Why must millions be doomed for hundreds of years to live and die without the slightest possibility of knowing anything about him? The plain answer to this is naturally that nobody knows; we are not in the secret. We do not know why there should be millions of years of life upon this planet before ever *homo sapiens* appeared. We do not know why one man is so brilliantly endowed and another is of rather low intelligence. We do not know why some men's skins should be darkly pigmented, or why some men's faces are yellow and others pink. We do not know why there should be races of men who are pygmies and races of men who are tall in stature. Life as we know it is full of inequalities and apparent injustices, and to claim that one particular piece of history is improbable because it appears to be unjust does not seem to me to be reasonable at all. It is like saying that electricity is improbable because men were obliged for so long to live without its benefits and facilities! The 'timing' of events, discoveries, developments, and revelations are not subject to any law of probability of which we have knowledge. If we can believe that there is a Divine Wisdom working out a total pattern extending far beyond our own short-sighted view, we shall not be quick to say that a unique event is untrue because it is 'improbable'.

I am not here concerned to argue about the historicity of the person of Jesus. For even if the records were scantier than they are, it seems to me quite inconceivable that a movement as vigorous and revolutionary as early Christianity could have sprung out of a myth. No one in his right senses denies the authenticity of most of the letters, or epistles, included in the New Testament, and several of these are considerably earlier documents than the gospels of Matthew, Mark, Luke and John. It is obvious from even a superficial reading of these human unselfconscious letters that people were being transformed in outlook and character, despite the general collapse of moral values in the pagan world. We may very properly ask the critic of the Christian story by what power were such transformations effected in such places as Corinth and Ephesus. Paul of Tarsus was undoubtedly a man of strong personality, but it certainly does not make sense to suggest that such radical changes in human character were made by the personal impact of one man. It is even more unthinkable that the weapons of such persuasion should be drawn from wishful thinking or a piece of calculated deceit. Can anyone seriously suggest that a man of Paul's not inconsiderable intellectual powers should lose his 'prospects' and wreck his career for the sake of something which never really happened? Is it reasonable to assume that such a man would write to the Christians at Corinth and quote as witnesses of the Resurrection of Jesus several hundred people who were still living at the time? (Does that surprise you? I suggest that you read the fifteenth chapter of the first letter to Corinth in modern English, remembering that it was written in about AD 56.) Can anyone really account for the audacity, assurance and endurance exhibited by the young Church without admitting that these early Christians were convinced that Jesus really rose from the dead? No one could honestly read the letters of the New Testament without becoming aware that not only the writers themselves but scores of other people were looking at life and death in a way in which they had never been looked at before, and were experiencing a contact with the living God unprecedented in human history. No one could fairly deny that in the first century AD something unique and remarkable had happened and that the letters spontaneously record its repercussions on human personality.

I find that people frequently forget the great value of these early pieces of evidence. They will quite readily suggest that the gospels were written-up stories of a departed hero, composed some time after his death. But they forget that the letters, which are real letters written to real people, reflect a phenomenon which has somehow got to be explained. What had any of the early Christians to gain by subscribing to an acted falsehood? Yet we find them willing to endanger their livelihood and their lives, prepared to undergo hardship, humiliation, persecution, torture and agonising death, simply because they were convinced that Jesus had really risen from the dead. Naturally all turns upon whether this 'resurrection' really and objectively occurred. The claims of Jesus to represent the character of God, his claim to be the master of men and of their ultimate destiny, and his claim to be sent by God to effect the reconciliation between man and God would remain as the lunatic arrogance of a disordered mind if everything ended in the judicial murder of a field-preacher on a Roman cross.

Chapter Eleven

THE CRUCIAL ISSUE

The Resurrection of Jesus is plainly the crux of the Christian faith. I must therefore remind the reader of some important points in the issue.

1. Those who have taken the trouble to study the evidence closely and exhaustively have frequently reached the conclusion that the events described, somewhat disjointedly in the gospel narratives, and in 1 Corinthians 15, did in fact take place. One famous example of a trained mind seeking the truth behind the Resurrection stories is that of Mr Frank Morison, whose thoroughgoing attempt to disprove the Resurrection ended in his own conviction that Jesus really rose from the dead. His well-known book *Who Moved the Stone?* is valuable and lasting evidence of the result of honest enquiry. But Mr Morison is not the only first-class mind to come to accept the truth of the objective Resurrection of Christ. The trouble is that so many have pre-judged the issue. They have already decided that the whole story may be dismissed as mass-hallucination, for example, and they never give their serious adult critical attention to this, the most significant of all human events.

2. Those who would explain away the Resurrection of Jesus by saying that he never really died, but revived in the cold of the tomb, leave themselves with insuperable difficulties. The practical impossibility of removing a body from a sealed rock-tomb guarded by Roman soldiers, conveying it to a place of safety and recovery, and re-establishing the resuscitated body as the Leader who has 'risen from the dead', seem to me to present far more difficulties than does belief in the recorded story. Is it really possible to

believe that the young Church as it moved into action was founded upon a swindle? Can it be seriously maintained that a dispirited group of disillusioned disciples were permanently transformed into a close-knit fellowship of spiritually resilient heroes by a concocted story?

I have grown convinced that more often than not it is sheer ignorance, sheer lack of study of the actual records, which makes clever as well as foolish men say, 'Well, of course, he was a great teacher, but I cannot accept the claim that he was divine.' For such a remark completely fails to account for the joyful certainty, courage, confidence and tenacity exhibited by the young Church. Unless we are prepared to deny the historical evidence altogether, all these qualities spring from one unforgettable demonstration – that after a public execution Jesus Christ rose again from the dead. To the early Church this well-attested fact proved his claims to the hilt.

3. According to the records the appearances of Jesus were extraordinarily unlike the apparitions seen by disordered minds. There was no atmosphere of expectancy or even of hope, and several times his sudden appearance struck his followers not with reassurance and joy but with a very natural terror. (Who among us could bear with equanimity the experience of watching our greatest friend publicly executed on Friday and then of seeing and hearing him alive and well on the following Sunday?) On one occasion at least (Luke 24:41) Jesus insists on the disciples' proving to themselves that he is not a ghost or an apparition. 'Feel me and see,' he said, 'ghosts don't have flesh and bones as you can see that I have.' And when their minds still could not react properly to what had in fact happened he asked for food – for everyone knows ghosts don't eat! We can imagine their frantic dash to the shelf for food, and all that they can find is a piece of cooked fish and part of a honeycomb. It is not until he has begun to eat this strange meal of fish and honey before their eyes that they realise that he is unquestionably alive – that he has conquered death as he had said that he would.

4. It is worth remembering that behind our ostensible reasons for believing or not believing a thing there are often unconscious reasons which go very deep. There are undoubtedly some who know intuitively how much depends upon the historic truth of the Resurrection. Should they once admit it to be true that this earth has been visited by the Creator, then the standards and values of the man who was also God will inevitably challenge and judge their lives. To some minds this must on no account be allowed to happen, and every ingenious argument and every literary resource must be employed to avoid the unwelcome conclusion.

5. Since most people have not studied the New Testament with their adult minds, and probably have not read it as a whole for many years, they are only too ready to accept someone else's disparagement of the Christian position without going to the trouble of examining the relevant documents for themselves. I think I may claim to know these records pretty well after many years spent in translating them into modern English. And I will say simply that in consequence I have become a hundred times more convinced of their authenticity than when I began the work. After even a moderate familiarity with these brief and sometimes almost naïvely simple documents, it becomes impossible to dissociate Jesus the ethical teacher from Jesus who claimed to reveal the character of God, who quite naturally forgave sins and who spoke with authority about human life, death and the world beyond death. We may, if you wish, allow that he was sometimes imperfectly reported, and it is certain that we have a very inadequate 'coverage' of the most important life the world has ever seen, but the more one studies these brief and incomplete records, the more unthinkable it becomes that they should be mere human fabrications.

For the New Testament as a whole speaks with a new certainty. God is no longer the distant unknowable Mystery; his nature and character have been revealed through a man, Jesus Christ. It is now known for certain that God's attitude towards mankind is one of unremitting love. The Master Plan which exists beneath the superficial activities of human beings is now becoming intelligible to them. The reconciliation between the holiness and perfection of God and the selfishness and evil of men has been unforgettably demonstrated. Death, the old dark bogey, has been exposed and resoundingly defeated. And as if this were not enough Good News for human beings to accept, they know now, by the acted parable of the Ascension of Christ, that God and man are eternally inseparable. Humanity is assured of its entry into the timeless life of God. A new dignity has been conferred upon the whole human race for God himself has become a man. New exciting possibilities appear as people begin to understand that the purpose of God's descent to the human level is to enable them to rise and live as children of God. And what is more, God is prepared to enter human personalities by his own Spirit to make such dreams come true. This temporary life is seen to be no more than the training-school for a purpose that points to dimensions beyond the confines of time and space. The centre of gravity of the new faith is not in present earthly activity but in a person and purpose far transcending it.

If Christianity today has degenerated in some quarters into a dull and spiritless moral code, that must not blind us to the tremendous fact upon which all Christian churches are founded. What could be more exciting than to know that the very feet of God have walked this earth of ours, that his authentic voice has spoken to men like ourselves? It is on this issue that we have to make up our minds and adjust our hearts. The Good News may have to be rescued from the encrustations of tradition, the confines of caution, and the dullness of familiarity, but *it is still there!* The historic fact remains, and, we in the twentieth century, with a conception of God infinitely greater than that of any previous generation, may have to short-circuit the centuries and let the startling truth break over us afresh – that we live on a visited planet.

Chapter Twelve

RETURNING TO THE SOURCE

The reason why I have said such things as, 'Forget about the churches for the moment,' is simply because I think that an entirely new, unprejudiced grasp of the God-man relation is essential for our generation. Experience has shown that such words as 'Christianity' or 'religion' or 'church' already have certain stereotyped associations in some people's minds. This 'conditioning' is frequently quite enough to insulate them from the shock of what early Christians believed – that God had visited this planet, that he had joined mankind permanently to himself; that he was no longer the remote and extraneous Power, but the Spirit who was their vigorous, intimate contemporary in the business of living. But it must be understood that by this insistence on a direct return to the great act of God on which Christianity is founded, I am by no means implying that all modern churches have lost their vision or reduced the revolutionary Good News to dull orthodoxy. I am quite sure this is not so, but I am equally sure that since modern man, for various reasons, is almost completely out of touch with the life and activity of the alert contemporary Church, he must be urged to go back and consider the act of divine initiative on which all Christian conceptions finally rest, before he can fairly observe any contemporary Church.

If we allow our adult intelligence and imagination to consider such a situation as at least *possible*, the value and significance of the Creator's visit to this planet become hard to exaggerate. We should have certain and reliable information about the character and personality of God, about the purpose and meaning of this life, about values and principles by which man can live usefully and happily, and about physical death and what lies beyond it. We should learn something of the underlying purpose beneath the shifting human scene, and how we could co-operate with it; we should learn how we could make the best of this limited imperfect world and how men could best prepare themselves for the next stage of their existence. In fact, the more we think about it the more valuable would be the information which we could obtain from the Creator if he focused himself in a human being.

Naturally we find ourselves wishing that such a person could be alive and accessible to our own age, prepared to answer our innumerable questions and solve our bewildering modern complexities! We might think it desirable that such an incarnation of the divine should appear in human life at least once a century, but the moment we begin to indulge in speculation like that we are falling into a line of thinking which leads nowhere. And even if we do come to accept as historic fact this planned focusing of God, it is plain that many of our eager modern questions will not receive the kind of detailed answer we might expect. A life lived for a mere thirty years in a poor occupied territory, itself of small account within the huge Roman Empire, would seem at first sight to be so narrow in outlook and hedged in by circumstance as to provide very little that is valuable for our modern perplexities. What is more, when this unique event took place, hardly anyone knew what was happening, and from the modern point of view a most maddeningly incomplete biographical record survives. Traditional piety and reverence have often made men reluctant to admit the paucity of information. In the recorded life of Jesus not a word has been preserved, for example, about his years of adolescence and early manhood. Yet these are times of painful and difficult adjustment for many human beings, and it might well be thought that a divine example would have been a help to many. Again, since Jesus was unmarried and was executed while still a young man, we are provided with no divine exemplar for the good marriage, for the successful coping with the problems of middle age, or for the gracious acceptance of the closing phases of earthly life.

But perhaps we are looking for the wrong things. Perhaps what we should look for is not so much a perfect pattern of living for every human age-group, but a revelation of truth which will illuminate the heart and centre of human life and give it a new significance and purpose. Perhaps we should be looking not for detailed answers to our many questions but the authoritative statement of the principles which govern life beneath the ebb and flow of human circumstance. Perhaps the information which we so earnestly seek will be both timeless and of universal application. Perhaps we shall to some extent be taken into the Creator's confidence, and yet handed back a great deal more of responsibility for decision than we bargained for!

I do not myself believe that anyone who studies with an open mind the records which we have of the life of God-become-man is likely to be disappointed. He may be surprised, mystified, or even taken out of his depth. The information he receives and the total impact of the personality whose life is recorded in the gospels may astonish and disturb him; it may even lead him to look at life from an entirely different point of view. It is only the one who relies on some sentimental recollection of gentle Jesus, meek and mild, who in later years discards what he thinks is the Christian faith. In my experience I have never known a person to make an adult study of this extraordinary life and remain wholly in the dark.

When, therefore, we do examine these records with serious attention, we do well to remind ourselves that the setting is, in a sense, unimportant. To my mind it will not necessarily help us very much if we study Palestinian customs or the Jewish religious system. It is far more important that we should realise that we are seeing God living life on human terms; God, in Dorothy Sayers's memorable phrase, 'taking his own medicine'. We are reading about something which had never happened before in the life of this world, and we can hardly expect the writers of the first century AD fully to grasp the significance of what they are describing. I have grown quite convinced of the substantial accuracy of their writing, but I cannot help sensing, beyond what was written, an actual awe-inspiring event, whose full implications we are only now beginning to understand. This may seem a strange and even arrogant statement to make, but what I am trying to say is that while the writers of the New Testament could hardly find words strong enough to express the certainty of their belief in Christ, the Son of God, yet their historic closeness to him and their very limited mental, and even geographical, horizons were bound to restrict their full appreciation of what had happened.

Within their limits of knowledge and experience there can be no doubt that the early Christians lived with sure knowledge of the living and contemporary God. And sometimes they showed the most remarkably inspired vision. Men like Paul could see the unlimited potentialities of the new situation which God had created. He could write such amazing things as these:

> Everything belongs to you! Paul, Apollos or Cephas; the world, life, death, the present or the future, everything is yours! For you belong to Christ, and Christ belongs to God!
>
> (1 Corinthians 3:21b–23)

> All of you who were baptised 'into' Christ have put on the family likeness of Christ. Gone is the distinction between Jew and Greek, slave and free man, male and female—you are all one in Christ Jesus.
>
> (Galatians 3:27–28)

> For God has allowed us to know the secret of his plan, and it is this: he purposed long ago in his sovereign will that all human history should be consummated in Christ, that everything that exists in Heaven or earth should find its perfection and fulfilment in him. In

> Christ we have been given an inheritance . . . So that we, in due time, as the first to put our hope in Christ, may bring praise to his glory!
>
> (Ephesians 1:9–12)

> Now Christ is the visible expression of the invisible God. He was born before creation began, for it was through him that everything was made, whether heavenly or earthly, seen or unseen . . . He is both the first principle and the upholding principle of the whole scheme of creation.
>
> (Colossians 1:15–17)

> In my opinion whatever we may have to go through now is less than nothing compared with the magnificent future God has in store for us. The whole creation is on tiptoe to see the wonderful sight of the sons of God coming into their own. The world of creation cannot as yet see reality, not because it chooses to be blind, but because in God's purpose it has been so limited—yet it has been given hope. And the hope is that in the end the whole of created life will be rescued from the tyranny of change and decay, and have its share in that magnificent liberty which can only belong to the children of God!
>
> (Romans 8:18–21)[1]

Nevertheless, despite the wonder of this prophetic vision, as we read the New Testament we may sometimes be conscious of a vast and timeless energy confined within the thought-forms and restricted knowledge of the first century AD. Today the experience, knowledge and responsibility of every thinking man is very much greater than that of most of the men of New Testament days. But what changed and inspired those men, what gave them daring, hope,

[1] These quotations are from the revised translation of J.B. Phillips, which he made in 1972.

patience and self-giving love is quite timeless. There is no real reason to suppose that we cannot tap the resources of God just as effectively as they did – no real reason except our modern insulations! If we could but see it, God is inevitably contemporary.

Chapter Thirteen

CHRISTIAN REVELATION

Now if we regard all real religions as attempts to get at a special kind of truth to provide some answer to man's intuitions about his own nature, we shall, I believe, find that what we know as 'Christianity' comprehends, develops and fulfils all that at heart we hold to be true. In a way that we should not have guessed, or indeed planned, God has visited this planet, and we can do no thinking or philosophising, nor can we deal with any human problem unless we take this fact into our serious calculation. It is perfectly true that the most convinced believer in God's focusing of himself in Christ does not 'know all the answers'. But at least he has enough true light by which to live, and he has powerful and indeed exciting clues to the meaning and purpose of life and to man's ultimate destiny. In order to make this clear I will mention some of the unique truths with which Christianity presents us.

1. With the coming of Christ a completely new God–man relationship came into being, which is not found in any other religion. Man enjoys a new value, a new dignity and new potentialities, because God became a human being. At the same time, man's conception of God is revolutionised by the thought that the Spirit of Wisdom, Love and Power behind all that we know, and all that we do not know, reduced himself to the stature of a man.

2. It is not always realised how closely the life and teaching of Jesus links the life of man with the life of God. Two examples from the recorded sayings of Jesus will perhaps serve to illustrate this:

(a) A fundamental problem of all religions is the problem of 'forgiveness'. Man sins and fails, despairs and loses faith, and yet he must somehow be reconciled morally and spiritually with the absolute perfection of God. Only God can resolve this sin-guilt-suffering-death complex, and Christians believe, however their interpretations may vary, that 'God was in Christ reconciling the world unto himself'. But quite apart from this act of reconciliation it is most important to realise that Jesus declared categorically that reconciliation with God is an impossibility without reconciliation with man. He taught, 'If ye forgive not men their trespasses, neither will your Father forgive your trespasses' (Matthew 6:15). We can hardly overestimate the significance of this statement, or of the general tenor of Jesus' teaching, which would not allow any divorce between love of God and love of man. We may perhaps wish the situation to be otherwise, but as far as we are concerned this is one of the conditions, definite and inexorable, by which we have to live.

(b) As far as the records show, Jesus gave only one parable of the final judgment which all men face after the probation of this life. The criterion is neither religion, nor orthodoxy, nor respectability, but the way in which man has treated man. (*Vide* Matthew 25, verses 31 to the end.) In this altogether revolutionary way of looking at things, which is unique to Christianity, Jesus deliberately and precisely identifies man's treatment of himself with man's treatment of man.

Here surely is the true humanism. Because God has become man, all men are at least potentially sons of God. It automatically becomes a serious offence to injure or exploit other people, not because of some vague humanist values but because God has done man the unspeakable honour of identifying himself with the human race.

3. Now although Christianity leads human thoughts and aspirations far beyond the limitations of this present stage of existence, and is thus in a sense an other-worldly religion, it is also incurably earthly. Men may have their visions, but

they are required to work them out in the everyday stuff of human situations. There is no room for mystical escapism; we find God-become-man himself involved in the messes and miseries of the human situation and requiring his followers to do the same. A man whose life is united with the timeless life of God through sincere and intelligent faith in Christ becomes strongly aware of his eternal destiny, and all kinds of inexpressible hopes for the distant future begin to stir in his mind. But he has to learn and to act in this present world, accepting good-humouredly his physical limitations and a fair degree of spiritual blindness. He has to express what is spiritually true in the context of ordinary human relationships and ordinary human problems.

As might be expected from a religion which is not the product of any particular human way of thinking but the result of a planned revelation, Christianity is of universal application. It cuts across barriers of class, colour and sex, and has a message of equal importance to the wise and to the foolish. It is perfectly possible for men or women of any race, colour or culture to be whole-hearted Christians. And while Christianity's highest and deepest implications may tax the brains and moral courage of the most fully-developed personalities, it can also be accepted by the relatively simple and ungifted.

One of the reasons why it is imperative for us moderns to get back to essential Christianity is that we may realise afresh the revolutionary character of its message. We have forgotten its devastating disregard, or even reversal, of current worldly values, and have allowed what we call 'Western civilisation' or 'the American way of life' to become more or less God-fearing substitutes for the real thing. For when God made his strange invasion of the life of this planet, the little section of humanity into which he came was obsessed as much as we are today with the importance of such things as power, privilege, success and wealth. By revealing reality, by declaring the Kingdom of God, God-become-man undermined or exposed these false values. He taught, and his teaching is as difficult to follow now as it was then, that what is *apparently* happening may bear little or no relation to what is *really* happening. The reality, according to him, is the establishment and growth of a Kingdom of inner loyalty which transcends all human barriers. Therefore, the realisation of the existence of this Kingdom, working for its expansion, living according to its principles, and, if necessary, dying for it, is the real significance of man's temporary existence upon the earth. Jesus taught, and demonstrated in person, that the very things which the world values most highly are irrelevant and ineffectual in the dimension of permanent reality. He neither denied the existing world nor despaired of its inhabitants, but by setting up an entirely different standard he showed the way of constructive human living. He showed men how loosely they could sit to this present world, how they need be neither deluded by its glamours, nor confined by its limitations.

It is particularly interesting to notice that he who was born a Jew cut fearlessly across the fierce Jewish prejudices of his day. It is for example well worthwhile studying his treatment of women and of the under-privileged. Quite as remarkable is his habit of being unimpressed by what was, and is still in some quarters, regarded as a sign of God's favour and the peak of human achievement – the possession of property and riches. It is because the teaching of Christ (which I believe to be the truth breaking through into a world of false values), is at once so realist, so disturbing and so revolutionary, that we need to go back to it with adult minds and hearts.

The moment the truth dawns upon us that the purpose of God's visit to this planet was not to establish another religion but to reveal the reality behind the appearance of things, we see what I believe to be another unique feature of the Christian Faith – its utter inescapability. Its principles and laws do not merely apply to religion and the religious way of life, they apply *to life itself,* wherever and whenever it is lived. For Christianity, although it is a religion in the sense that it links the life of man with the life of God, is far more than one of the world's great faiths; it is the revelation of the way of true living. Since, unless we live as hermits, we are all to a greater or less extent bound up with each other, we cannot escape behaving towards people or treating people in one way or another. And because Christ has plainly declared that the way in which we treat people is a mirror-image of the way in which we treat God, the most ardent atheist or thoroughgoing agnostic can no more escape from Christianity than he can escape from life itself. You cannot contract out of life, and since God has personally visited the planet, you cannot contract out of the reality which underlies the business of human living. To me at least this is not a 'religious' matter at all; it has not necessarily anything to do with going to church, or praying, or reading the Bible, or even of believing in God. It is a matter of the quality of our living, and God's assessment of that no one can ultimately escape.

It is taken for granted in the recorded teaching of Jesus (and in the New Testament generally) that this life is lived against a background of what can literally be translated as 'the life of the ages'. The present business of living is merely a prelude, acted in the time-and-space set-up on this planet, to life in another dimension where present limitations do not obtain. It is probably impossible to describe the next stage of existence in earthly terms, and it would be childish to take literally the picture-language of the New Testament writers who make some attempt to hint at its unimaginable splendours and possibilities. But the teaching of Christ is that the ultimate destiny of human beings, as far as we can at present comprehend it, is not extinction or absorption into the Infinite, but the full development, the bringing to maturity, of sons of God. For all we know, there lie ahead of us activities and responsibilities far beyond our present dreams, but at least it is clear that what we do in this present life is a significant factor in determining our status in the next. It is unwise to press parables too literally, but the general tenor of the parables of Jesus emphasises man's moral responsibility in the here-and-now, the certainty of life persisting beyond physical death, and the equal certainty of his continued co-operation with the joyful purpose of God – or his exclusion from it. Therefore, although Jesus would be the last person to use fear as a moral weapon (except in the case of the desperately self-complacent), he did teach that life should be lived with a due sense of awe and responsibility. I believe he did this not merely because of man's short- or long-term effect upon others, but because of his destiny in the dimension which follows what we call 'death'.

Now this background of 'eternity' is absolutely essential to any reasonable belief in God. Without it the glaring injustices, the inexplicable tragedies and the unsolved problems of this life make nonsense of the idea of a loving God. But if we have here only the preparatory stage, the first working-over of the raw material, the significant beginnings but not the final endings of a vast purpose, we can accept life with a much better grace. We are no longer tortured by the dreadful limitations of man's life on this planet, and while as lovers of God and lovers of man, we are bound to do all that we can to spread the invisible Kingdom here on earth, we know that both the foundation and the fulfilment of that Kingdom lie beyond the confines of our present situation. Why this should be so we simply do not know. Indeed, it is only one of the hundreds of known facts about human life which we must accept with a proper and reverent agnosticism.

Chapter Fourteen

SOME CRITICISMS OF CHRISTIANITY (1)

A great many criticisms of the Christian faith, as has already been suggested, are not valid criticisms at all. The critics have never taken the trouble to study what the faith really stands for, and in most cases have certainly never studied the relevant documents, namely, the books of the New Testament, with their adult intelligence. For example, it is only too easy to imagine Christian living as a soft, meek-and-mild, head-in-the-clouds avoidance of reality, and therefore to pour scorn upon it. But no one could seriously read the essential message of the gospels, or study the lives of the early Christians without seeing that living according to the plan of God calls for the highest courage, and makes the most strenuous demands on the human spirit. Again, it is, alas, still possible for otherwise intelligent people to jeer at Christianity as a 'pie-in-the-sky' religion which has little or no contact with day-to-day life. But could anything be more devastatingly practical than the way of living outlined by Jesus, and followed since by all kinds and conditions of people? Could sane people really study the records of such men as Paul and Luke, and say that theirs was an escapist religion? Or, for that matter, could anyone read of what Christians are doing today to combat fear, ignorance and disease in the dark places of the earth, and still say that a faith which impels them to do such things is either a drug to their sensibilities or a means of escape? It is not worth trying to answer the criticisms of those who have neither taken the trouble to find out what is involved in embarking on this way of living, nor even to observe the lives of those who have followed it faithfully.

Nevertheless, quite apart from the ill-informed attacks upon something which never was the Christian faith, there are some legitimate criticisms, made by sane and thoughtful people, which must be considered. For example, there are those who are filled with admiration for Christ's demonstrated way of self-giving love, and of his personal non-resistance to the forces of evil. But in practice they may have serious doubts about the efficacy of such methods. Here we need to do some careful thinking, for many of the current ideas of Christ are not true to the character revealed in the gospels. In others words we have to see with clearer eyes what love in action really entails. While it is true that Jesus offered no resistance to physical attacks against himself, his love did not prevent him from using the most aggressive and blistering invective against those who thought they held a 'corner' in religion. For all his loving-kindness, he did not hesitate to say that a man who led a little child astray would be better off dead. He roundly declared that such notorious evil cities as Sodom and Gomorrah would fare better in the judgment than towns which rejected the living truth when it was before their eyes. He was no verbal sentimentalist; he was not prepared to gratify King Herod's whim to see him 'perform', but bluntly called him a fox. He was moved to violent physical action by the combination of irreverence and black-marketeering which was corrupting what was meant to be the centre of worship – the Temple in Jerusalem. Thus we must not over-simplify the issue and say that in a given situation the attitude of Christian love must always be that of meek acceptance and the patient smile. The schoolmaster in charge of forty or so tough adolescents in one of our big cities cannot mediate the love of God without its sternness. It would indeed become impossible for a policeman, a detective or, shall we say, an inspector of the NSPCC to be a true Christian at all if our concept of the way of love were limited to that of passive acceptance or non-resistance of evil.

Now here we strike one of the really fundamental

problems of the way of love, a problem of which not every clergyman and minister appears to be aware. It is a fine and moving thing to advocate the way of patient love from the pulpit on Sunday, but it is quite a different thing to apply that love in the complex situations which arise every day in the shop, the office, the garage, the workshop, the laboratory and the factory. For the Christian is not merely concerned about himself; indeed he may rightly feel that in following his Master's example he may have to accept as patiently and as good-humouredly as he can anything from a personal slight to sheer injustice *as far as he is concerned*. But he is not only concerned with himself, and that is just where the task of interpreting the way of love becomes difficult. Is the Christian to stand wordlessly by while someone else is bullied or unjustly treated? Is the Christian to say nothing when corrupting suggestions are made? Is the Christian to give silent assent to practices which he knows are dishonest? It is here, in the very stuff of life, that men and women so frequently and so wistfully abandon their dream of being 'loving' to all men. Surely much more thought and honest discussion between Christians is needed on this point, as well as a more realistic appraisal of the actual demonstrated methods of Jesus. And we have to admit that it is just here, in the painful issues of actual human relationships, that clergy and ministers have sometimes been unable to give sound advice.

As soon as we begin to study in earnest the recorded actions of Christ, we cannot help being struck by his extraordinarily varied approach in dealing with different people. It is immediately apparent that no rule of thumb is applied, but that the purpose of constructive love is very flexible in the face of human complexities of character. Thus, one person may best respond to the most uncompromising challenge, while another needs patient encouragement. One is told that his life already approximates in pattern to what God is wanting him to be; but another may be told bluntly that despite all his religious profession he is at heart a 'child of evil'. It is only when we detach 'texts of Scripture' that there are apparent contradictions in the sayings of Christ. Once we grasp the underlying principle of love in action touching human lives in various states of awareness and development, we can begin to understand why so many different things were said to so many different people.

Now if we turn from the life of Christ to our ordinary experience of people, most of us would probably agree that there are certain types of men and women who need to be shocked or jolted out of their self-love and complacency before they can begin to see and appreciate what true and constructive love is trying to do. It is impossible, for example, for the schoolmaster to lead his pupils into the appreciation of what is good and true and beautiful, unless he has first established discipline. Those who have been most successful in rebuilding the character of juvenile delinquents know that their work would be impossible without love, but that such love must be a stern love, particularly at the beginning. If Christian love is supposed to be 'doormat-like' in its meekness and gentleness, in many existing human situations it does not have a chance to get started at all. Now these words are far from being an argument for what was once called muscular Christianity, but they are a plea for an honest examination of real situations. The need to use physical force, the need to bring people slap up against the consequence of their own wrong-doing, and sometimes the need to deflate them drastically are undoubtedly called for by certain human situations, but as methods they are only part of a much bigger whole. Such means may make it possible for true concern to be shown and for reformation to begin. But the actual constructive work of changing a situation or reforming a character can only be achieved by understanding and love.

With such considerations in mind we begin to see that the scathing denunciations of religious leaders, which are quite a prominent part of Jesus' recorded sayings, belong only to the first part of the process of love. Christ needed to use violent methods to crack the armour of complacency.

(And it is not always remembered that such attacks did not invariably result in increased hostility. Some at least must have had their spirits stabbed broad awake by such aggression, for we read in Acts 6:7 that 'a great company of the priests were obedient to the faith'.) If therefore as Christians we feel obliged to use the reprimand, the *argumentum ad hominem,* or even physical restraint, we must realise all the time that such things are only a means to an end; by themselves they are both incomplete and ineffectual. They can do no more than provide the proper conditions for the constructive patient work of love. The schoolmaster's work of establishing discipline is only a prelude to the positive self-giving task of real teaching. The policeman's arrest of the wrongdoer is only the prelude to the patient reformation of character. Christ's apparently merciless attacks upon complacency were no more than the initial stage of the work of God's Spirit upon the personalities of the men behind the façade.

Chapter Fifteen

SOME CRITICISMS OF CHRISTIANITY (2)

A further apparently legitimate criticism which is sometimes levelled against the Christian faith is that it depends entirely upon an old-fashioned conception of God and upon the assumption that this little planet is the centre of the whole universe. Modern astronomy has forced many to realise how frighteningly vast is the universe of which we have some knowledge; and that, for all we know, there may be countless other universes, at present beyond range of our means of observation. Many therefore find it inconceivable that the Mind behind this bewildering creation could reveal the essence of his character in a unique life lived on this almost negligible planet. We can sympathise with this difficulty. It is a great deal more acute today than when the Psalmist meditated on the relative insignificance of man, and wrote, 'When I consider thy heavens, the work of thy fingers, the moon and the stars, which thou hast ordained: what is man that thou art mindful of him?' (Psalm 8: 3, 4) – simply because man's scientific knowledge has been very greatly extended. But whatever mistakes the Christian Church may have made in past ages of intolerance, surely no modern Christian is concerned to maintain that the revelation of God given to this planet which we inhabit is necessarily the only revelation God has made in his whole universe! We simply do not know what creatures may exist elsewhere, and therefore we cannot begin even to guess at other kinds of revelation which the Creator may have given, or may plan to give, in other parts of his apparently limitless creation. In spite of the fragments of knowledge concerning the nature and size of the universe which science is continually gathering, we need constantly to remember that our primary concern is, whether we like it or not, with the earth on which we live. It is what God has revealed to *us* which is important to us, and surely our most pressing and most urgent problems are concerned with life on this planet. We are not God; the fact that we 'cannot imagine' the Creator's total purpose for the whole universe proves nothing except the limitation of our own capacity to comprehend. Further, although our minds are so made that they are necessarily impressed by almost unthinkable size, by energies at which the imagination boggles and by aeons of time which we cannot in any real sense appreciate, there is no reason to suppose that outside the human mind such things are of any great significance.

A further objection which is sometimes made to the Christian faith lies in its claim to uniqueness – that it is in Christ alone that God has revealed his personality and character. The impartial observer knows that Christianity is only one of the world's religions, and that for millions of people other faiths appear to suffice. Surely, it may be argued, if there is only one God the object of worship in all religions is the same, and it cannot greatly matter how that worship is given or what means are used to regulate human life in accordance with the divine purpose. Such criticism usually comes from those who know very little about either Christianity or other religions. Obviously there are certain basic goodnesses which are urged by any religious system, and equally obviously any religion which is sincerely believed in will have individual and social effects. The modern Christian, whatever follies the Church may have committed in the past, does not deny the value of all true religion. Shafts of divine light, of truths not discoverable by 'scientific' means, have broken through upon the human scene through poets, philosophers and sages, as well as by the founders of various religions. This fact no intelligent modern Christian would minimise, but such fragments of revelation can, he believes, be only secondary to the planned personal focusing of God in the man Jesus Christ.

Indeed the more seriously he takes his own faith, the less it seems to him that its overwhelming significance has so far been rightly appreciated. If, as the Christian believes, God has actually entered the human scene then there is an inescapable uniqueness about Christianity. If this is 'the real thing' then in a sense there can be no compromise with anything less. This does not mean lack of sympathy with other religions, but it does mean a determination that all men shall know the fullest possible truth.

Another objection to the Christian faith which is felt, if not expressed, by many intelligent people is that it appears to attract the immature and seeks to perpetuate their immaturity. By insisting that men 'become like little children' and that they accept life at the hands of their 'heavenly Father', Christ appears to be placing a premium upon childishness and tacitly disapproving of men's growth towards more mature conceptions of the world. Now this objection needs careful and honest answering. It is perfectly true that there is a divine simplicity about Christ's teaching which is more readily grasped by the uncomplicated than by those whose minds have become so 'cultured', 'conditioned' and 'educated' that they are blind to the prime conditions of human life upon this planet. Therefore, Christ says in effect, if men are to grasp the purpose of God they must begin again to learn as children. Now it is inconceivable that the One who was God-become-man should deprecate the pursuit of truth or despise human knowledge; and it is equally unthinkable that he wished to inaugurate a movement limited to members of low intelligence! Surely the force of his remarks is that there must be a return to humility in the God–man relationship before human knowledge and the acquisition of truth have any real meaning. A moment's reflection will show us that there is a fundamental difference in the mental attitude of the learned man whose faith is in humanity and that of the learned man whose basic faith is in God as Creator and in man as God's creation. Jesus is concerned to establish the fact that compared with the immensely complex wisdom of God we are children, and that until we accept that fact with humility our knowledge will either be a burden to us or may lead us further and further from essential truth. It is true that some Christians are childish, and that some remain in a state of arrested development. It is even true that some Christians are finding in God a 'father-substitute' and seeking to perpetuate their own dependent childhood. But that is not true of the personality of Christ nor of any mature or effective Christian from Paul onwards. Nevertheless, I believe that Jesus was perfectly right in insisting that *compared with God* we are dependent, incomplete and liable to all the mistakes of childhood; that is one of the given facts of the human situation, and the wise man recognises its truth.

Another stumbling-block of the Christian faith which presents itself in various forms to the modern scientific temper of mind is that the truth of such faith is not susceptible to scientific 'proof'. I must confess I often wonder what sort of proof the scientifically-minded are asking Christians to produce. Let us freely admit that organised Christianity has made tragic and repeated mistakes. We could go further and say that in some centuries and in some countries the Church has borne only the slightest resemblance to the life and teaching of its Founder. But if we look away from the failures and consider the effect on character and personality of a genuine Christian faith, surely we are presented with something very impressive. We have already mentioned the zeal and vigour of the early Christians and the undoubted historical fact that the direction and quality of people's lives were dramatically changed in New Testament days. But if we skip the centuries for the moment and come to modern times, there is plenty of evidence of a similar faith producing a similar effect. Within my own experience I know scores of people to whom God has become a reality through their intelligent acceptance of the Christian faith, and who know experimentally that the resources of God are available to sustain and invigorate human spiritual life.

Now if, as I have suggested, Jesus Christ came to inaugurate a new way of constructive living, it is obvious from what we know of human nature and of the human situation generally that there will be a very considerable pull-back to easier, safer, and more comfortable ways of living. The small-scale and large-scale failures of Christians down the centuries – and they are many and grievous – are no indication at all as to what the Christian faith, honestly received in heart and mind, can achieve. And it is quite unrealistic to judge the validity of the Christian faith by assuming that such European countries as Britain, France or Germany are 'Christian'. For various reasons, not least I think because men and women of influence have failed to take the Christian revelation seriously, the actual number of convinced and active Christians is, even today, quite a small minority. If we are looking for 'scientific proof', then, of the truth of the Christian faith, let us look at genuine Christians and not at the actions of any nation which is only nominally Christian, nor at any Church which has again and again acted in a spirit completely contrary to that of its Founder.

But by far the most serious criticism comes from those who would sincerely like to believe the truth of Christianity but find the very nature of life itself appears to deny it. The idea of God as a loving heavenly Father, who marks the fall of every sparrow, appears to break down in the complex stresses, disasters, inhumanities and horrors of modern life. There appears to be a certain winsome simplicity about the Christian view of life which has to be reluctantly discarded when we grow up and face both life and people as they are. I believe there are many people to whom the teachings of Christ are true in the sense that a vision or an ideal is true. It is with real regret that they see the vision and ideal daily destroyed by man's greed, inhumanity and fear. I believe that such people are wrong. If they were to return to study the gospels again, they would find no evading of the issues of human exploitation, injustice and persecution, no avoidance of life's inequalities, injustices, evils and disasters. But I understand their unwilling discarding of the Christian faith – for the problem of human suffering and evil is without any doubt, for most people, the greatest barrier to belief. And while no one can hope to solve it satisfactorily and completely there are several considerations which should be carefully examined, by which I believe it is not impossible to see life fairly and squarely, and at the same time to be an honest Christian. But for such considerations, we must have at least a separate chapter.

Chapter Sixteen

PROBLEMS OF SUFFERING AND EVIL (1)

'If there is a God of Love,' people have asked and are still asking, 'how can he allow so much suffering in his creation, how can he permit natural disasters such as earthquakes, and how can we possibly reconcile the existence of evil with the idea of an all-wise, all-powerful, all-loving God?' What are commonly called the 'problem of evil' and 'the problem of pain' are inevitably the most serious problems which face anyone of intelligence and sensibility.

Let it be said straight away that no one knows anything like the full explanation of, or the answer to, these problems. The most we can do is first to break the problems down into what can partially be answered and what cannot, and secondly, to suggest an attitude of mind which can be honestly held without the necessity for denying the existence of a God of Love. Anyone who writes on this, the hardest of all human problems, must write with humility. For although he may himself have experienced a little of the burden of human suffering, and although he may have observed a very great deal more in other people's lives, he knows that there is no easy answer. If he has seen almost unbelievable courage and endurance and, what is even more moving, an unshakable conviction of the final goodness of God, he is bound to feel humble. He knows that, although he may write about the problem, there are countless thousands who could never write books but who in practice have met and solved the problem in a way that no words, however wise, could do.

Our first consideration should be to recognise that evil

is inherent in the risky gift of free will. Naturally it is possible for the Creator to have made creatures who are invariably good, healthy, kind and virtuous. But if they had no chance of being anything else, if in other words, they had no free will, we can see, even with our limited intelligence, that such a creation would be no more than a race of characterless robots. It is really no good quarrelling with the situation in which we find ourselves, and quite plainly that situation includes the power to choose. And it is obvious that this individual gift of being able to choose good or evil affects a far wider area of human life than that of one individual personality. The good that a man chooses to do, or the evil that a man chooses to do, have both immediate and long-term effects, and exert an influence, even spread an infection, of good or bad. Speaking generally, human life is so arranged that what we call 'good' produces happiness, and what we call 'evil' produces misery and suffering. Thus a good deal of human suffering can be directly traced to the evil choices of human beings. Sometimes this is perfectly obvious and direct – a violent and cruel husband plainly causes suffering, fear and misery to his wife and children. Sometimes the evil is indirect – the greed for money or power may make a business man take decisions which bring great suffering to hundreds of people personally unknown to him, or the selfishness and greed of one generation may produce a bitter fruit in the next.

If we knew all the facts, and the effects, both short-term and long-term of human selfishness and evil, a very large proportion of mankind's miseries could be explained. But of course this in no way answers the questioner who asks, 'Why doesn't God *stop* evil and cruel men from causing so much suffering?' This is a very natural and understandable question, but how exactly could such intervention be arranged without interfering with the gift of personal choice? Are we to imagine the possessor of a cruel tongue to be struck dumb, the writer of irresponsible and harmful newspaper articles visited with writer's cramp, or the cruel and vindictive husband to find himself completely paralysed? Even if we limit God's intervention to the reinforcement of the voice of conscience, what can be done where conscience is disregarded or has been silenced through persistent suppression? The moment we begin to envisage such interventions, the whole structure of human free will is destroyed. Again, may I repeat that we may not approve of this terrifying free will being given to men at all, but it is one of those things which we are bound to accept. (It may be worth pointing out here that the whole point of real Christianity lies not in interference with the human power to choose but in producing a willing consent to choose good rather than evil.)

The next problem which must be squarely faced is the apparent flagrant injustice in the distribution of suffering. (I feel bound to use the word 'apparent' because I do not believe in final injustice, as I hope to show later.) Put in its crudest form the question is simply, 'Why should the innocent suffer and the wicked get away with it?' This is one of the oldest questions in the world, far older of course than the Old Testament book of Job, which makes some attempt to deal with it. It is true that even within the limits of this little life people do sometimes see virtue rewarded and wickedness punished. But unhappily for their sense of justice, this is by no means invariably the case. To all appearances the cruel people with hard faces have a much better time in this world than the good, the sensitive and the responsible. Now here again we come right up against the situation in which we find ourselves, and which we must to some degree accept. There can be nothing wrong with our desire for justice, and there can be nothing but right in our desire to see evil restrained and exploitation cease. But if we are expecting a world, and blaming God for not supplying such a world, in which good is inevitably rewarded and evil automatically punished, we are merely crying for the moon. We are not living in such a situation, and indeed it is debatable whether adult virtue and courage could exist at all in such a kindergarten atmosphere. This life *is* unjust, in this life the innocent *do* suffer, and in this life hard conscienceless people *do*, to all appearances, 'get away with it'. These are hard facts and only to a limited degree can we alter them.

Frankly, I do not know who started the idea that if men and women serve God and live their lives to please him then he will protect them by special intervention from pain, suffering, misfortune and the persecution of evil men. We need look no further than the recorded life of Jesus Christ himself to see that even the most perfect human life does not secure such divine protection. It seems to me that a great deal of misunderstanding and mental suffering could be avoided if this erroneous idea were exposed and abandoned. How many people who fall sick say, either openly or to themselves, 'Why should this happen to me? – I've always lived a decent life.' There are even people who feel that God has somehow broken his side of the bargain in allowing illness or misfortune to come upon them. But what *is* the bargain? If we regard the New Testament as our authority we shall find no such arrangement being offered to those who open their lives to the living Spirit of God. They are indeed guaranteed that nothing, not even the bitterest persecution, the worst misfortune or the death of the body, can do them any permanent harm or separate them from the love of God. They are promised that no circumstance of earthly life can defeat them in spirit and that the resources of God are always available for them. Further, they have the assurance that the ultimate purposes of God can never be defeated. But the idea that if a man pleases God then God will especially shield him belongs to the dim twilight of religion and not to Christianity at all.

But it helps enormously, indeed it makes a fundamental change in our thinking if we look upon the life we lead upon this small planet as temporary, as only part of a whole, the quality and extent of which we can only very dimly perceive. For the purposes of life the Creator has made certain conditions, but we have no reason to suppose that the same conditions apply in the stages of life we live after the death of the physical body. It is largely because people today have lost the sense of what we might call the background of eternity that they see everything from pleasure to pain in terms of this world only. Yet if they were seriously to accept the attitude of mind which prevails throughout the whole New Testament they might come to see that, although there are many things which appear to deny the love and justice of God in this life, they are quite literally *in no position* to judge the final issue. If they try to do so, they might easily be as foolish as a man attempting to determine the pattern of a carpet from examination of a single thread, a picture from a tube of paint, or a book from a box of assorted type. At most they are only seeing the raw beginnings of something so enormous as to stagger the imagination.

Naturally, it is easy to pour scorn upon the conviction common to all true Christians that, as Paul put it, 'the sufferings of this present time are not worthy to be compared with the glory that shall be revealed in us'. It can be called 'pie in the sky', the 'opium of the people', and doubtless it has been used as an anodyne for much preventable human suffering and exploitation. But the true Christian does not so use this point of view; he uses it to stabilise his own thought. To my mind, and I say this most seriously, it would be impossible to believe in a God of love and justice if the human horizon were limited to this life only. But the Christian's faith does not rest in the here-and-now, and even at best he knows he is only seeing a little piece of the total picture. He knows, to put it crudely, that God's love, mercy and justice must be infinitely greater than his own! Therefore, while he works on hopefully and cheerfully in this imperfect stage of existence, he never expects to find anything approaching the final working out of God's purpose within the confines of life on this planet. He lives in the incomplete, the undeveloped, the inexplicable and the mysterious. He has enough light to live by, but he never claims to know all the answers, and throughout his life he is sustained by the conviction that he is moving towards the complete, the perfect and the real. He is destined for light and enlightenment, for freedom from illusion, release from his present blindness to reality and from the inevitable limitations of his physical nature.

For many people natural disasters such as earthquakes, floods, hurricanes, erupting volcanoes and all the other destructive forces of Nature produce an insuperable obstacle to faith in a loving God. There is naturally no easy answer to explain such occurrences, but there are some considerations which make the problem a shade less difficult. A fertile valley in the United States of America was disastrously flooded, not for the first time, a few months before this book was written. Nevertheless, the commentator in the film showing scenes of this disaster remarked that, although the area had been flooded again and again, within a year or two of each catastrophe, people would quickly forget and resettle in the same area. Similarly, people will live under the shadow of a volcano which is known to erupt violently and unpredictably from time to time. It may sound harsh to say so, but a certain proportion of human life could be saved if areas known to be dangerous for human habitation were avoided, or the proper steps to control the forces of Nature were taken where this is possible. Man is mistaken if he thinks life upon this planet is automatically physically safe. But he has been given powers of body and mind and qualities of forethought and the ability to profit by experience. It would seem to be part of his job to learn to control the enormous energies of Nature. We still have not the slightest idea why the situation should be as it is, but the blackness of what we call 'natural disaster' is made far darker than it really is because of modern man's obsession with physical death as the worst evil. Moreover, we persist in viewing disaster through human eyes. It is only from the human point of view that the headline, 200 KILLED BY EARTHQUAKE – 5,000 HOMELESS is more distressing than, FARMER KILLED BY LIGHTNING, WIDOW PROSTRATED BY GRIEF. The question, 'How could a God of Love allow *so many* to be killed and so many to suffer?' has really very little sense in it. *We* may need the impact of a large-scale piece of human suffering before we are properly impressed, but in the eyes of the sort of God whom Christians worship, the question of number and size is neither impressive nor significant, impossible as it may be for us to conceive the concern of God for the individual. To imagine that God looks upon physical death as many men and women do, or to think of him as impressed by numbers, violence or size, is simply to think of God as a magnified man – a monstrously inadequate conception.

Now the one who has the attitude of mind which is rooted in eternity is neither deceived by the illusive glamours of this world nor unduly cast down by the unexplained suffering and the unsolved problems which confront him on all sides. This does not mean to say for one moment that the true Christian regards his passing through this life as a somewhat boring prelude to the glories that lie ahead. Indeed, as a follower of Christ, and as one whose life is aligned with the purpose of God, he is inevitably involved in the life of this world. He is committed to do all within his power to heal the world's injuries by active and outgoing love, and the personal cost to himself is probably high. He is not less concerned than the materialist or the scientific humanist for human welfare, but more so; for he has glimpsed something of a person's value and potentiality in the eyes of God. But all the time he enjoys the enormous advantage of knowing that even the most hideous suffering only exists in this present state of affairs. He knows that death need be neither a disaster nor an enemy. He never suffers from the frustration of believing that this little world is any more than a visible beginning of some incalculably vast plan of the Creator. In short, he is much more likely to see life in proportion than the one who insists that life on this planet sets the final boundary of human experience.

It is a great help in facing life to believe that the final answers, the ultimate outcome, can never be settled in this particular phase of our existence. Of course, to the person without faith this appears to be both a piece of evasion of real issues in that it shelves difficult problems, and a piece of wishful thinking in that it believes in the ultimate goodness of God in some nebulous hereafter, even though the daily evidence of life denies such goodness and love. It is probably quite impossible to explain the Christian attitude to the thoroughgoing materialist, simply because the major premise which makes the whole position tenable and satisfactory is *God*, and the materialist denies such a person's existence. But, speaking as one who did not arrive at his present convictions without a good deal of questing and questioning, I would assure the materialist that his position looks every bit as ridiculous and untenable to the man who has some small knowledge of God as the Christian position does to the materialist! The materialist appears to be speaking and arguing not only in ignorance of a whole dimension but with a colossal if unconscious arrogance. For he is really wanting to comprehend the total scheme of things with the mind of the Creator. He appears to forget that we are not yet 'Old Boys' who can talk on familiar terms with the Headmaster! We are all very much still at school, and probably very junior members of the school at that. Further, although we may not be able to convince the materialist, the Christian does not adopt his supra-mundane point of view wilfully, as a kind of escape from life's hard realities. On the contrary, once he finds himself aligned with the vast and complex purpose of God the new point of view is born in him, and to go back and hold earth-limited views of the problems of pain and suffering appears as absurd as to believe that the world is flat. You cannot deny a new dimension once you have experienced it.

But while the Christian believes that God is a wholly reliable 'shelf' on which unsolved problems and difficulties may for the time be safely deposited, he does not find himself in any way excused from attempting to relieve suffering and pain and to play his part in rebuilding the true order amid the chaos of earthly conditions. He is inspired by the recorded example of God-become-man who, without arguing about the 'givenness' of the human situation, set about healing men's disorders in a most down-to-earth fashion. Yet the Christian is not relying merely on a nineteen hundred years' old demonstration for his day-to-day inspiration and reinforcement, but on a living contemporary Spirit. He is no longer envisaging 'God' dwelling in unapproachable remoteness and making impossible demands of man whom he has placed in a difficult and perplexing condition. The living God is allied to us, is with us in the fray, not merely guiding and encouraging, but striving and suffering and triumphing with us, in him and through him. So that even though the centre of gravity of the Christian's faith is not really in this world at all, yet as far as this life is concerned God is always his contemporary. At any given moment in history there is bound to be a large number of questions without any satisfactory answer. In the face of this, a great many people adopt an attitude of non-committal agnosticism. So long as their questions remain unanswered, they feel in no way morally bound to co-operate with such good purpose as they can discern. This is a characteristically modern attitude; for in past centuries people had to take for granted the fact that a great many of their *hows* and *whys* would certainly remain unanswered in their lifetime. Yet this did not prevent them from acting boldly and resolutely along the lines which they were convinced were right. But people of today, perhaps a little intoxicated with their success in answering the *hows* of life, will frequently not commit themselves until their *whys* are answered – in fact, until the Creator has taken them into his full confidence! Thus in dealing with the real human problems, such as the relief of suffering, the adjustment of personality, the release from fear and ignorance, the care of the physically or mentally defective or of the aged and infirm, there is nearly always a desperate shortage of living agents, and among their small number the cosily non-committed agnostic is very rarely to be found. I would suggest that since we are in a very junior position in the universe, we might do better to set our hands and hearts to tasks that cry out to be done, instead of posing everlasting *whys* before we are willing to work to alleviate human suffering and needs.

Chapter Seventeen

PROBLEMS OF SUFFERING AND EVIL (2)

Some of the physical 'evils' in the world are plainly inimical to human life and constitute a continual challenge to human vigilance and ingenuity. We have made enormous strides in discovering the causes of disease, and are still fighting a long drawn-out battle against such things as the incredibly minute viruses, and the apparently arbitrary cell-degeneration known as cancer. Of equal importance with these discoveries is the increasing knowledge of the influence of the mind upon the health or disease of the body. A vast amount of further experiment and correlation of experience is needed in this field. Before long more emphasis will be placed upon curing a disease by working from the inside out, so to speak, that is, by paying far more attention to the condition of the centre which controls the functioning of that organic whole which we call the body. But again, though we may hope for many significant answers to our *hows*, we have no answer at all to our *whys*. *Why*, for example, should the virus of poliomyelitis exist at all? Or *why* indeed should there be disease, not merely in human beings but throughout the whole animal creation? Some of our ancestors were apparently satisfied to believe that the whole army of bacteria, germs and viruses which lie in wait to injure or destroy human life were the direct consequence of the sin of Adam. Naturally it is possible to concede that the breaking of natural laws, as for instance those of health and hygiene, can incur natural penalties, but surely it surpasses even the most vivid imagination to suppose that one man's disobedience to, and defiance of, his Creator, could actually *create* deadly organisms and viruses! Moreover, when it is known from the malformation of bone structure of animals which existed a very long time before humans appeared on the earth that they also suffered from disease, the argument falls flat on its face. We still have no clue whatever as to *why* what we call 'disease' should exist at all.

To connect human disease with human sin is an easy and obvious, but to my mind, misleading thing to do. It is altogether too facile an explanation and is contradicted by the evidence every day. We can probably all think of people who live good and unselfish lives yet suffer from disease. And we can also think of people who are thoroughly self-centred who are full of energy and have not had a day's illness in their lives! Indeed it would appear that there is a monstrous unfairness about the incidence of physical disease. I am well aware that certain kinds of functional disorder and even actual disease are being more and more frequently alleviated and cured by increasing the health of the human spirit, and I regard this as a most hopeful approach to the whole question of healing. But that does not alter the fact that, as one looks upon life dispassionately, those in rude health are for the most part extroverts who feel no particular concern for the world around them, while those who suffer from poor health and an assortment of diseases are often sensitive, conscientious people who are doing what they can to lessen the world's sorrows.

Although we are quite in the dark about the *why* of human disease and suffering, ordinary observation can show us that the *result* of their occurrence is by no means necessarily evil. It is not in the sentimental novel only that the self-centred husband has been shocked back into responsibility, and even into a renewal of true love by the sickness of his wife. Similarly the illness of a child can and does renew and deepen the love between a husband and wife. And I can recall quite a number of occasions when visiting in hospital men who had never previously been ill in their lives, being told that such a forcible withdrawal from life came to be regarded far more as a friend than as an enemy. 'It gives you a chance to think.' 'It makes me think about myself and what I'm in this life for.' 'It's made me think about God and pray to him for the first time since I was a kid.' 'It's opened my eyes to a new world – I just didn't realise that this sort of thing (that is, suffering and nursing care), was going on all the time.' 'I didn't know what human kindness was till I came here (that is, into hospital).' These are only a few typical remarks made to me in recent years, and they far outnumber those of the self-pitying or embittered. What is even more impressive and moving is the almost super-human courage, hope and faith shown by the human spirit when the body is attacked by pain and disease. I am sure that disease is in itself evil, but I am left wondering how the courage, love and compassion it evokes would be produced in a world where everybody was perfectly healthy. Perhaps physical health is not of such paramount importance as our modern geocentric materialist would suppose.

This question of the physical evil in the world leads us naturally on to the question of moral evil, which poses at least as difficult a question, even though it is sometimes argued that they are but different manifestations of the same thing. It is customary nowadays to look upon evil as either the absence of good through ignorance or fear, or else as something which manifests itself through maladjustment of personality. It is not considered to have any objective reality. I believe this to be as fallacious a point of view as to look upon disease as the mere absence of health. It is certainly true that the healthy body, controlled by the healthy mind, will successfully resist all kinds of disease-producing organisms. But this does not prove that the organisms do not exist, for their objective existence can be demonstrated to anybody's satisfaction. I believe there is a valid parallel here. The fact that moral evil is defeated by the spiritually healthy human being does not prove the non-existence of moral evil.

We have unfortunately grown accustomed to the monstrous inhumanities and cruelties of our modern world. Shocked as we have been by well-attested stories of unspeakable tortures and degradations, by the mass exterminations of the gas-chamber, and by the living death of such places as Belsen, many people found it difficult to react with proper indignation to the later cruelties of the Communist slave-camps in Siberia, or the callous indifference of most people to the plight of millions of refugees. It is as though human sensibility has been dulled by repeated shocks, and has even come to accept the most revolting barbarity as an inescapable part of the modern human scene. In time of war we may perhaps say that men revert to the impulses of primitive savagery, and this may well be true. But no savage, however primitive, can show the cold, calculated ruthlessness of so much that has happened in recent wars. This is not a question of going back to the fight for survival, to 'nature red in tooth and claw', but the appearance of something infinitely more radical and sinister. This is not 'the growing pains of civilisation', but the premeditated use of terror, degradation and vicious brutality.

How are we to begin to explain the existence of such evil? It is not the case of a few maladjusted personalities exhibiting anit-social tendencies; it is like some frightening moral infection which can basically affect thousands, if not millions, of people. *But where does it come from?* Admittedly I have drawn attention to large-scale suffering, but the question is just as difficult to answer when we come to the hatred, lust, malice, greed, pride and selfishness which mar the national, social and family life of our own country. It seems to me quite inadequate to regard the qualities which spoil relationships as mere absence of good, and for myself I am driven to the conclusion that there is such a thing as evil which can infect and distort human personality just as certainly as there are germs and viruses which attack and damage the physical body.

It is clear, at least to me, that people who worship and

love the true God, and open their spirits to the active Spirit of Love, show to a greater or less degree the presence of good within them. It does not seem to me therefore unreasonable to suppose that those who worship and love the wrong things create conditions whereby they are actuated, and to some extent possessed, by 'evil'. In fact, although it may sound old-fashioned, I do not believe that we take the question of 'evil' seriously enough in modern days, so that we are continually being disappointed, shocked or horrified by its manifestations. Although I am very far from subscribing to the doctrine of the total depravity of man, it does seem to me to have been proved within my own lifetime that the problem of human evil is not much affected by better education, better housing, higher wages, holidays with pay, and the National Health Service – desirable as all these things may be for other good reasons. We need a much more realistic approach to the problem of human evil, and I am perfectly certain that no really effective way of dealing with it will be found apart from the rediscovery of true religion.

When we come to examine the life and teaching of Jesus Christ we may at first be surprised to find how little explanation he gives of the human situation. He does not argue about the existence of suffering or evil, still less does he seek 'to justify God's ways to man'. He does not appear to waste time in arguing about the desirability or otherwise of the human situation. He accepts it and he concentrates upon the centre to which everything else, however important or impressive, is merely peripheral. That centre is, of course, the human heart, or perhaps we might be more particular and say that inner centre of human personality, where the very springs of action are conceived. As we study the admittedly incomplete records of that unique life, we shall see that his particular genius lies in concentration upon what is really essential. The deep fundamental problems of human life are really neither intellectual nor technical; they are always in the last resort problems of human relationship. It would seem that Jesus (regarding him for the moment purely as a man of poetic insight), could quite easily disregard the nonessentials, the mere trappings and scenery of human life. His concern was with the quality of human living, and in his eyes aspects of our human life, which appear to us of pressing importance, were of little significance to him. It might indeed be fair to epitomise his whole attitude in his own famous words, 'What shall it profit a man if he gain the whole world and lose his own soul?'

Now this refusal to be influenced by non-essentials never meant in Christ's life an indifferent pietism. For although it is plain from his life and teaching that he looked upon this life as a prelude to something infinitely more important, yet, wherever it was possible, he restored health of mind and body. He was deeply moved by the strains and distresses of men, by their hunger and thirst and weariness, and he was roused to passionate indignation by the exploitation of the weak. Indeed, he alone of all religious leaders of all time was bold enough to state, as we saw above (*vide* Matthew 25, verses 31 to the end), that love of God must be expressed by love of man, even in his earthly and sordid distresses. For although Christianity is an incurably other-worldly religion and speaks unhesitatingly of sharing the timeless Life of God, it is also devastatingly practical and down-to-earth. It holds out the highest ideals and promises, and yet faces life with a downright and almost frightening realism. If we regard Christ seriously as God-become-man we shall find his reaction to the life around him extraordinarily illuminating. Yet he offers no explanation of the origin of evil or of human sin and suffering. No doubt he used the language of his own day – it would be difficult to know what else he could have done – but surely there can be no doubt that behind such expressions as 'Satan', 'the Evil One', 'the Prince of this world', 'Beelzebub' and 'the Devil', there is recognition of the power of evil. His concern was not to explain how such a power came into existence, but to defeat it. It seems probable that we shall have to share this attitude and spend our energies, not in discussing the origins of evil, but in defeating it, both in ourselves and in the world around us.

Now I venture to suggest at this point that we need resources outside ourselves to defeat this evil. So long as we cling to the idea that we live in a closed-world-system, the most we do is adjust and rearrange existing forces. But if it is true that spiritual energies of constructive good are really available in a dimension of which we know very little, surely we are very foolish to ignore them. We should know by now that 'Satan cannot cast out Satan', and that although force may restrain evil it is powerless to transform it into good. We probably all know from experience that the only quality which has patience and strength enough to redeem either people or situations is the quality of outgoing love, the very thing of which we are all so lamentably short. If, again, we look at God-become-man we find that as a matter of course and of habit he opened his personality to God, not merely to be sure that he was following the divine plan of action but to receive potent spiritual reinforcement for the overcoming of evil. If this was necessary for him we might sensibly conclude that it is even more necessary for us. And yet how few, even alas among professing Christians, deliberately and of set purpose draw upon the unseen spiritual resources of God? We are so infected by the prevailing atmosphere of thought, which assumes that nothing can enter our earthly lives from outside, that a great deal of what the New Testament takes for granted does not strike us as realistic or practical. Yet I would suggest that there are discoveries to be made here which would prove far more revolutionary in the solving of human problems than any purely physical marvels.

Chapter Eighteen

THE CHALLENGE TO LIVING

There is a tendency in most of us to avoid the most crucial and painful issues. This is perfectly obvious in the weak character who, in common parlance, 'takes the line of least resistance'. But even in characters whom we should call 'strong', that is, in properly integrated, mature and purposeful people, there is frequently a reluctance to decide upon radical spiritual issues. A well-disciplined human character will seek with determination the solution to a 'scientific' problem, or deal courageously with the complexities of a political or 'business' situation; many people are capable of exhibiting the highest qualities of courage and endurance in the face of terrible physical handicaps and dangers. But it remains comparatively rare for a person to be willing to fight the spiritual battle, to put into practice the principle of outgoing love which is the heart of Christianity. The moment we begin to come within range, as it were, of the danger area a great many people take refuge in what I can only call 'cosy agnosticism'. For so long as a man can persuade himself that he may honestly maintain an open mind about the identity and person of Jesus Christ, he remains uncommitted to the real business of living. Since he has no real standards he can be tolerant in isolation instead of becoming embarrassingly involved. Since he is unenlisted in any supra-human purpose, he is free to give or withhold himself as he chooses. Since he owes loyalty to nothing but his own humanist ideals, he is under no personal obligation to touch or be touched by the evil he deplores. And since he is responsible to no one, he need feel no particular guilt or failure in avoiding battles in which he can observe a pitiful minority struggling ineffectually. This attitude of non-committal detachment is one of the most crippling evils of our time. Of course, there are thousands of people who, with the greatest moral courage, are coping with the sufferings, evils and distresses of our common social life, but if we come to examine any of these human efforts to deal with human needs, there is almost always a desperate shortage of dedicated men and women. 'Dedicated' is the operative word, for so long as people have no faith in any value or purpose beyond the immediate human situation, there is nothing, in the last analysis, to which they can be truly dedicated. People may be 'nice', honest and kind within certain limits, but nothing is going to break the cosyness of agnosticism except a resurgence of faith. It is absolutely necessary for us to recapture the sense that this limited human life is surrounded and interpenetrated by a timeless spiritual dimension. Christ spoke unequivocally about 'coming from' the Father, and 'going to' the Father. It was said of him that 'he went about doing good and healing all manner of sickness and disease among the people'. He claimed that the work which he did, whether it was the healing of body, mind or soul was the work of God himself. Yet at the same time he stated quite definitely that his 'Kingdom is not of this world'. In other words, while he operated within the time-and-space situation, and neither despised nor detached himself from actual human living, he lived in continual awareness of what, for want of a better word, we call 'eternity'.

We may think his free use in the parables of the ideas of rewards, compensations and punishments in 'the life to come' somewhat crude. We like to think that we do good for the sake of doing good and not for any reward or through fear of any punishment. But if we take Christ seriously we cannot avoid the conclusion that our status in the next stage of existence will be largely determined by our behaviour in this one. As far as I know Christ nowhere suggests that we should be 'good', unselfish and loving merely because we shall thereby win a heavenly reward.

Nor does he suggest that we should avoid evil merely because we shall otherwise suffer for it hereafter. He is simply concerned to state what he clearly sees to be inevitable consequence; he is neither threatening nor promising, but stating inescapable fact. His chief call therefore is to what is usually rather misleadingly translated 'repentance', actually to *metanoia,* which means a fundamental change of outlook, the acceptance of a quite different scale of values. The call to follow him, to enlist in the service of his Kingdom, must sooner or later include this revolution in thinking. It is really a call to freedom, freedom from the preoccupation with self, and from the preoccupation with the values of the closed-system of this world. It is as though he were showing people something of their true dignity and destiny – he is revealing the fact that they are all potentially, and may become actually, children of God. He exposes the play-acting (that is, the hypocrisies) of human living, its lovelessness towards fellow-men, and its blindness to the contemporary presence and purpose of God. In effect, he calls them to a new pattern of life, the way of self-giving love, which is not shaped by earthly caution and prudence, but guided by his own living Spirit. It is a call to heroic and adventurous living, dangerous and exciting. For it is nothing less than the following, in this present level of living, of the timeless pattern which extends far beyond it. It cannot be contained by the old forms and traditions, and, as he himself remarked, any attempt to put the new wine into old wineskins would be disastrous.

Now it does seem to me that, in an age which has done and is doing exciting things in almost every department of life, this call to a new and true way of living should have a wide appeal. We have come to equate the supernatural with the 'spooky' and the spiritual with the nebulous. But suppose we ourselves are being called to a *metanoia*. Suppose we are asked to believe that the dimension of ultimate reality is only partially adumbrated by what we see happening in human life? Can we not, on the authority of the historic Visit, make at least a leap of imagination and see our lives as a temporary indication in time and space of something of far greater value and significance? Must we be so geocentric in our thinking? Can we not see that it is only from our point of view that this life looks like the whole? Could we not for a moment forget to be 'sensible' and 'scientific' and believe that our dreams, our longings and our intuitions, which can never be satisfied in this life, are not vapours of wishful thinking, but quietly insistent reminders of our true destiny?

Now although Christianity is an 'other-worldly' way of living in that it derives its values, its power and ultimate purpose from a source outside this planet, it is, as we have seen above, incurably earthly. Therefore, we must not be surprised, if we embark on the course of following the way of Christ, to find that we are at once challenged by mundane difficulties. It is no good pretending that the way of freedom, of true insight, and of deep joy is some painless primrose path. If it were so all men would unquestionably by now have become devoted followers of Christ. The way of living which recognises God as the centre of life instead of the self, or the aggregate of selves which we call humanity, does carry an endorsement of truth, but not without arousing hostility both inside and outside ourselves. We do not realise the depth of our former blindness, or the distortion of our previous values until we begin to live by the Light of the world.

We are in fact called to a battle, a battle which is largely a matter of holding tenaciously to what we inwardly know to be true in spite of apparent contradiction. But however sharp the conflict may be, no one who has seriously put his faith in Christ's revelation ever wants to go back to a blind and purposeless existence. The Christian holds a clue to the meaning of life which is a pearl of very great price, and he will never let it go. It is true that he is faced by problems of every kind, by strains within and without himself, but he is no longer walking in darkness, and he knows that he is not walking alone. At the best he sees life and its purpose with such clarity that he is amazed that all cannot see and embrace the truth; but at the very worst, whatever life may inflict upon him, he knows himself to be indissolubly joined to the reality which is God and he is in no doubt about the ultimate outcome. Following the way of real living may prove costly and difficult; but I know from my own experience and from that of many others that it provides increasingly a sense of satisfaction which is almost indefinable. Something very deep within us knows that we are in harmony with the real pattern, the real purpose – we have begun to live as children of God.

I see some clue to the spiritual satisfaction afforded by acceptance of the Christian faith in what have now become established as the psychological essentials of human living. For the distilled wisdom of psychological schools of thought really amounts to this: that human beings need above all love, security and significance. The personality deprived of any of these three, especially during the formative years, is inevitably bound to show signs of inner deprivation. To put it in plain terms, everybody needs to love and be loved, everybody needs a reasonable degree of security, and everybody needs to feel he holds a significant place in human society. A great many human evils are directly attributable to the fact that people have been or are deprived of these basic requirements. Now the conscientious humanist society will do its utmost to meet these psychological needs, but I believe that they must also be recognised at a much deeper level, at the level of the naked and lonely human spirit. Because many people live most of their lives in the company of others, and indeed many cannot bear to be alone, these deep needs are often concealed. But when circumstances force them, possibly through tragedy, bereavement or personal suffering, to realise their solitariness, a need far deeper than the basic psychological requirements is, often poignantly, experienced. Man finds that he needs both to love and be loved *by God,* not in any sentimental sense, but at the centre of his being where pretence is impossible. He desperately needs real security, not physical security, for life has probably taught him that comparatively few can enjoy this, and in any case, sooner or later, it is knocked from their grasp by the fact of death. He wants the deep security of knowing that he is in fact a child of God, and that there is nothing whatever which could possibly happen to him which can affect the ultimate safety of that relationship. Spiritually, too, he deeply needs to know that he is of value, that his little life is significant in the vast eternal scheme of things. Properly understood, the Christian faith answers these needs at the deepest level. Countless men and women have in their own darkness and solitariness found that there is 'someone there'. In the God revealed by Christ they discover love, security and significance of a quality inexpressible in words.

But there is no need to wait for life to strip us of our armour and reveal us to ourselves in our solitariness. We need not wait till the superficialities are destroyed before we make a determined plunge beneath the surface to find the meaning and significance of life. God, I repeat, is inescapably and at all times contemporary.

Chapter Nineteen

THE MISSING DIMENSION

The longer we live the more life will reveal to us our inescapable loneliness, insignificance and insecurity. No one can be said to be living at all until he has realised and come to terms with the real and permanent which transcends change and decay. A man without the sense of reality underlying and extending far beyond present realities is, to anyone who has even glimpsed the dimension of true living, a deficient and pathetic figure. He may be brave, kindly and unselfish but he cannot escape being a clueless cardboard figure in a meaningless, purposeless world. I believe the time is coming when this geocentric conception of the human predicament will seem foolish and inadequate. I believe that as science discovers more of that unseen which 'programmes' and 'patterns' the seen, it will become more and more clear that physical death is not always a disaster and is never a finality.

I wonder why it should be thought unscientific to believe in the dimension of God, in spiritual forces and spiritual realities which have demonstrable effects upon people. An everyday example will show the illogicality of such thinking. We are surrounded by such things as radio, television, radar, X-rays, sunlight and the artificial lighting of our streets and homes. *All* these things produce or are produced by vibrations of various wavelengths in what used to be called the 'ether'. Now in spite of the fact that the wavelength of any of the above-mentioned phenomena can be accurately measured, and despite the fact that the speed of these vibrations through the 'ether' is known, it has become scientifically unfashionable to talk about 'ether' at all. These vibrations occur in 'space', and 'space' has the ability to support or transmit vibrations of widely varying frequency. Indeed, the radio-telescope can detect 'radio' vibrations from exceedingly distant stars whose light-vibrations cannot be received at all by any optical telescope in the world. Yet we are told that this medium which transmits measurable vibrations at a measurable speed has no objective existence; its function is simply a property of space. All right, then. But if we can swallow such a dictum of science without a murmur, why should the values and realities of the spirit be held to be unreal and imaginary? We might, for instance, suggest, in imitation scientific terms, that there are 'vibrations' of the human personality higher up the spectrum than our scientific humanists will allow. We might go further and suggest that these 'vibrations' are a property of the 'spiritual dimension' just as truly as the etheric vibrations are a property of 'space'. And it is really a poor argument to say that the existence and reality of the spiritual are purely subjective phenomena. For, after all, the result of every scientific experiment is ultimately a subjective one, since it is human beings who decide whether a theory is proved or not. There are millions of people today to whom the spiritual and supra-human are quite satisfactorily 'proved'.

The discovery of God, his purpose, the dimension of 'eternity' and all that follows from this experience seem to me to come along certain lines. And these, which I now mention, are based upon actual observed experience, although of course there must be many others.

(a) A man, for reasons that he certainly could not put into words, is dissatisfied with the atmosphere of non-faith in which he has been brought up. Unlike the noble souls who apparently find satisfaction in pursuing purposes in the certain knowledge that the whole universe is purposeless, he is oppressed with the futility of an ordinary human life. For some reason or another, and very often because he has observed the stability and satisfaction which a true religion has given to someone else, he begins to seek with an open mind. For the first time he reads and studies as an adult the documents of the New Testament. During this period of study he 'prays' and attempts to open his whole personality to God, if indeed there be one. This is normally a fairly slow process, but again and again I have observed such a man, or woman, discover the livingness of God. Christ steps out of the ancient pages and becomes an unseen but real contemporary person.

Now I would emphasise that in these conditions, which apply to quite a number of the Christians whom I know, there has been no outward pressure and no indoctrination. It is true that such Christians may later ask for 'instruction', so that their knowledge of this new truth may be deepened and widened. But in the first instance neither guilt, fear nor the pressure of anybody else's personality forced such people into religious faith.

(b) There has been in my experience a small number of people who came 'to seek God' almost in despair because they were defeated by their own temperaments, desires or circumstances. To put it quite bluntly, they saw themselves being pulled down by something either inside or outside themselves which they were growing less and less able to resist. Such people turn to God as a kind of last resort. I know several who found that the hitherto unexperienced God does in fact exist. They received, in varying degrees, an experience of reconciliation, and to some extent this may be explained purely in terms of internal psychology. But what I personally find so remarkable about such happenings is that men and women find in God a power greater than themselves, which is demonstrably available in their situation. It is naturally very easy for the clever and well-adjusted to sneer at simple people 'finding Christ', 'knowing the saving power of Jesus', and to forget that behind the 'corny' expressions that may be used there lies a rather awe-inspiring truth. For that which is theoretically unattainable is in fact attained: human nature is changed both in direction and in disposition.

Because this is a genuine experience of some people, it is only too easy for certain evangelists to assume that it is the right way for all. They therefore concentrate all their energies upon inducing a sense of guilt, and then presenting the message of salvation and forgiveness. Unfortunately it is only too easy, especially among young people, to produce this feeling of guilt. And once it has been produced sufficiently strongly, a personality may be led in almost any direction – a truth which is well-known to Communist indoctrinators. But in practice, and as a result of observation, the induction of guilt by methods of mass evangelism frequently has one of two unfortunate results. First, after the experience of having the feeling of guilt aroused and then tranquillised the person of intelligence may come to see how he or she has been emotionally exploited. I have known of people whose last state was thus much worse than their first because, having once got over the humiliating experience, they are thereafter suspicious of what true religion is trying to say. The second unfortunate result, and again I know this from observation, is that people may come to regard the guilt-forgiveness experience as the high-spot of the religious life. Indeed, it assumes such paramount importance in their minds that anything else in the complex business of living seems scarcely worth consideration. Consequently we find people clinging to their experience of being 'converted', 'saved' or 'born again', but quite obviously never allowing the revolutionary message of true Christianity to penetrate their thinking or their feeling. Fascinated by the wonder of their own 'redemption' they continue to live in a cocoon of forgiveness and let the world go hang.

(c) There are people, people of intelligence and integrity, some of whom at least have been nominal members of a church for many years, upon whom the truth seems to break in quite sudden illumination. This may happen through a study group, through a mission, through the ordinary ministry of the Church, through the reading of a book, or through personal conversation. The significance and relevance of Christianity, which had previously been dulled or impotent, becomes radiantly clear and strong. Words and phrases which were meaningless suddenly become alive and meaningful. Christianity is no longer just a reasonable hypothesis, but the truth by which all other truths are judged. God, vaguely believed in as a background power, becomes alive, operating in and through the contemporary scene.

(d) Then there are a few people whom I know (and I wish with all my heart that there were more), who have, apparently accidentally, discovered the relevance of the Christian faith to the work that they have been trying to do for humanity's sake. I can think of a probation officer, a male nurse in a mental hospital, a hospital sister, a youth worker, and some others who, over the years, discovered that they were unconsciously (or perhaps intuitively is a better word) following the way of outgoing love, which is the way of Christ. I have no wish to make exaggerated claims, but I think I can fairly say that in all these cases the sense of worthwhileness and purpose was deepened and strengthened when their work was seen to be part of the 'immemorial plan'. These people also gained in their personal lives because God became to them a living and active power instead of a vague possibility.

The above examples of a few people who have found God real and contemporary, and who have thereby gained a sense of purpose which far transcends this little life, are no more than a brief record of those whom I have personally known. Obviously, such experience could be multiplied by thousands, if not by millions, throughout the world. It is an undeniable fact of human experience that contact can be made with a reality beyond the visible realities. To me at least this is evidence for the existence of God which simply cannot, in common fairness, be lightly dismissed.

Now unfortunately for the scientifically-minded, God is not discoverable or demonstrable by purely scientific means. But that really proves nothing; it simply means that the wrong instruments are being used for the job.

God is discoverable in life, in human relationships, in the everlasting battle between good and evil, even though he may be conceived as transcending all these things. There is no discovery of the truth of Christ's teaching, no unanswerable inward endorsement of it, without committing oneself to his way of life. We can observe with detachment the failures of Christians and the virtues of non-Christians as though life were a competition in goodness, but we can never know for certain what life is really all about until we have honestly committed ourselves to the Christian way of living. The test lies in the doing, and as Jesus himself once said (I translate freely from John 7:17) – 'If any man wants to know whether this teaching comes from God or is of purely human invention, he must set himself to follow the purpose of God.'

Christianity is an invitation to true living, and its truth is only endorsed by actual experience. When a man becomes a committed Christian he sooner or later sees the falsity, the illusions, and the limitations of the humanist geocentric way of thinking. He becomes (sometimes suddenly, but more often gradually) aware of a greatly enhanced meaning in life and of a greatly heightened personal responsibility. Beneath the surface of things as they seem to be, he can discern a kind of cosmic conflict in which he is now personally and consciously involved. He has ceased to be a spectator or a commentator and a certain small part of the battlefield is his alone. Consequently, he also becomes aware, as probably never before, of the forces ranged against him. As in every evolutionary process, including the growth of a normal human being, there is a force which pulls upwards, but there is also a force making for relapse and regression. We must not be surprised to find a man whose eyes have been opened to spiritual reality experiencing again and again reactionary forces within himself. He is, I believe, being drawn to a higher level of human living, a greater awareness, and a greater responsibility. In the nature of things there will inevitably be a pull-back to the former, more comfortable, mode of non-committed thinking and feeling.

In addition to this tendency within himself he will in all likelihood be surrounded by many people who regard his new enlightenment as moonshine and will exert a day-by-day pressure to bring him back into line with 'ordinary' life. But there is a third factor of opposition which I attempt to define with some hesitation. For it appears to me, on comparing my own experience with that of many friends, that once one has seriously enlisted on the side of God and his purpose some considerable spiritual opposition is provoked and encountered. Quite apart from one's own tendency to regress and quite apart from the atmosphere of non-faith in which many Christians have to live, the Christian finds himself attacked by nameless spiritual forces. It is very easy for the non-committed agnostic, or indeed for any non-Christian to make light of an organised force of evil. But it is highly significant to me to find that in every case of a person becoming a Christian, of which I have personal knowledge, this sense of spiritual opposition is experienced, and sometimes felt very keenly. If we may personify the forces of evil for a moment, it would appear that 'Satan' does not bother to attack, for example, a University Professor of Philosophy, a popular film star, a busy farmer, a telephone operator or a worker in heavy industry, or anyone else, just so long as they are uncommitted in the real spiritual battle. There is no particular point in producing pressures of evil against a man or woman who moves harmlessly and respectably with the normal currents of contemporary human living. But should they once begin to embark on real living, to assist in the building of the Kingdom of God, then the attack begins. We may read C. S. Lewis's *Screwtape Letters* superficially with amusement, but if we are committed Christians, we know that the diabolical subtlety and ingenuity are no mere literary fancies.

To my mind, we are driven, if we are honest, into an inescapable personal decision if we are determined to know the truth. God remains unproven or a myth until we commit ourselves to the way of Christ. The forces of evil, 'the devil',

'Satan', and all such conceptions remain as a laughable superstitious hangover until we seriously attempt to lead Christian lives. I have therefore no hesitation in challenging any agnostic who wants to test the truth of the Christian faith. Let him commit himself and before long he will know both the splendour of the truth and the seriousness of the struggle.

Chapter Twenty

RE-PRESENTING CHRISTIANITY

I am sometimes inclined to think that what the Church of England, at any rate, lacks more than anything else is a proper means of disseminating information. Its pressing task is quite simply to tell people what the basic content of Christianity is, and to give them some information of what the Christian Church is achieving in the face of ignorance, fear, disease and sheer physical human need in many parts of the world. Since ninety per cent of the people in this country are never inside the churches, and since only a tiny fraction even of church-people regularly read any church literature, some means must be found of propagating true Christianity. This, I think, must mean buying newspaper and magazine space, making the fullest possible use of radio and television opportunities, employing highly-skilled professional journalists, establishing information centres and providing literature 'popular' enough to be available in the secular bookshop and bookstall. In fact, I believe we must seize every modern means of communication for re-presenting Christianity.

Of course such dissemination of information can never be a substitute for Christian living, for Christian witness to the truth and Christian ways of coping with human situations. I do not mean that at all; I am only concerned to point out the need for sheer elementary information. Such a work requires a very great deal of money as well as the highest gifts of imagination, insight and sympathy. But I remain convinced that it must be done and should command urgent priority. I have found that a prodigious ignorance about Christianity exists in all classes of people, but I have not always seen this recognised in church circles. Indeed I have often heard opinions expressed, at meetings of clergy and others, which assume that the people of this country are openly and defiantly rejecting the standards and claims of Christian living. I am sure that this is an entirely false view. A few random conversations with ordinary non-churchgoing people in different parts of the country quickly reveal that most people have only the haziest idea of what the Christian faith is all about. I am not sure that we are even living in a 'post-Christian' era. It would be far more true to say that our society is neo-pagan. For although it may well be that a certain brand of Victorian piety was rejected during or soon after the First World War, there has been no wholesale repudiation of the basic message of Christ. I do not know whether there would be, but at least it seems to me of the greatest importance that people should know, in terms which they can understand, what it is they are being asked to accept or reject. The stuffy materialism, the routelessness, the uncertainty about moral values and the collapse of belief in anything beyond the tomb, are not in themselves a rejection of Christianity so much as *cri de coeur* for the truth of the Gospel.

Now although it is true that in a sense the task of the Church is always the same, for it always means introducing something of the spiritual life of the contemporary God into a community, in another sense its work must differ according to circumstances. When Christianity began, the young Church sprang into urgent life in spite of the darkest and most discouraging circumstances. Our own circumstances may look dark and discouraging enough for the rebirth of true Christianity, but they differ almost *in toto* from those of the first century AD. If we read the New Testament documents we see that their background is largely one of fear, cruelty, superstition, corruption and a callous lack of consideration for human beings. The widest disparity between rich and poor aroused no censorious voice; slavery, exploitation and immorality of all kinds were commonplace, while a gang of more or less discarded gods and a bevy of *passée* goddesses permeated the common life of the countries surrounding the eastern Mediterranean. The only religion which maintained strict monotheism and upheld moral standards, and which might have proved a friend and helper, became a bitter foe. It is abundantly clear from the New Testament record of Paul's life that the Jewish religion, in which he himself was nurtured, proved as implacable an enemy to the new faith as paganism itself. In those circumstances the early Christians called men from faith in false gods to faith in the living God, from lives ridden by fear to a life lighted by the love of God. They called men from multifarious sins to a life of wholesome confidence, supported and reinforced by a God who actually pervaded their personalities. Perhaps above all they called men to share the timeless life of God so that they could regard their present lives as an almost infinitesimal part of an awe-inspiring and magnificent whole. The call was a definite one; it was from darkness to light, from fear to confidence.

The issue today in this country is nothing like so clear-cut. The vast majority of people are not living evil or depraved lives. There is still a public conscience of considerable strength ready to condemn greed, exploitation and cruelty. There is still a great deal of willing self-giving service which, when it is known, commands widespread admiration. The 'gods' and 'goddesses' which rule the lives of many of our people are not personified and cannot easily be denounced or dethroned. The growth of 'scientific' knowledge, to which I have referred many times above, coupled with the increasing urbanisation of our society, has destroyed primitive fears of divine justice either before or after death. Since the grosser sins are mostly avoided and apathy is not considered wrong except in time of war, most people are not oppressed with a sense of guilt or sin. It is a pagan world all right, but it is a very different world from the cruel, lustful, callous, violent world of two thousand years ago.

Somehow or another those of us who believe that

Christianity is good and relevant news for a bewildered generation have got to do some hard thinking about our methods of re-presentation. For example, there has never been a time when the value of human life has been so highly regarded and when what are loosely called 'human' values are the sole guiding principles for most people. This seems to me to offer a very great opportunity for Christianity to make its unique claim for the value of human beings. 'People matter' not simply because the nicest people think so or because humanists say so, but because God focused himself in a human being. Human values, instead of being variable and uncertain because they are established by human beings themselves, are revealed by God-become-man. The essence of Christian behaviour is to treat people as *people*, all equally loved by the same Father, however much they may differ in talents or development. But we must go far beyond mere humanism. It is not simply that the value of human beings has been established by an act of God, but that a huge far-reaching plan has been begun. The Kingdom of God, a Kingdom of inner loyalty, which has neither its roots nor its culmination in this temporary life, has nevertheless been established as an historic fact upon this planet. This Kingdom already exists, and its standards and methods of working challenge the life of everyone. A new dignity, a new importance and a new responsibility, have all been brought into the life of man. He can co-operate or he can refuse to co-operate with the patient way of love. He may or may not be religious, but since 'no man is an island' he cannot escape from the issue involved – he either helps or hinders. The refusal to be committed and the attitude of indifference can in fact never be neutral.

To re-establish this concept of the importance and responsibility of living means speaking with the utmost conviction and speaking repeatedly. This is no time for offering people completely out of touch with the Church a snippet of religious comfort or an isolated text from the Bible in some obscure corner of the daily or Sunday newspaper.

It is no time for assuming on the radio, on television or in any other public place that people have somehow carelessly lapsed from the Christian way. It is no use blaming people for failing to reach moral standards when many of them scarcely possess any definite standards at all. It is equally useless to belabour people for not attending public worship when they have only the sketchiest idea of what Christianity really means and even less of what the Church stands for. The time has come for the Church to restate boldly and unequivocally that the Way, the Truth and the Life have all been revealed, that the Kingdom is here already and that the battle in which there can be no neutrality is on. The bankruptcy of humanism without God should be ruthlessly exposed and its disquieting similarity to godless Communism deliberately pointed out. The added depth, the added dimension, which human life receives when linked to the timeless Life of God, should be fearlessly proclaimed. False gods do not exhibit their power or even their existence until the living God is experienced. Sin and failure have no meaning until the challenge of a new way of living is thrown down. Non-committal agnosticism is never seen as an avoidance of the responsibility of living so long as the truth remains unknown. No man knows the strength of the enemy until he has fully enlisted on one side or the other. People will never take evil seriously nor even see much need to tap the resources of God until they join in with the costly redemptive purposes of love.

We cannot, of course, command success, but we can, at least, present people with the truth as relevant, practical and rewarding in our modern life. We proclaim not a myth but a historic fact, not an idealistic pattern of behaviour, but an active, joyful way of living life. We do not preach a stoic courage in the face of life's ills and accidents, but an acceptance of living from a heavenly Father whose final purpose can never be defeated. Above all, we do not preach outworn pieties reeking of superstition and mediaeval misunderstandings, but honest contact with the living God. By sheer force of circumstance we are beginning to recover the good sense shown by Paul and many of the early Christians. We are beginning to see that this little world never has offered and never can offer physical security. We are beginning to see that the vast purpose of God can never be confined to individual salvation nor to the welfare of any particular race or nation, nor even to the necessarily restricted physical life of human beings on this planet. Perhaps, not without wonder and awe, we can at last see how bold and imaginative was the man Jesus when he called a few fishermen and others to found a worldwide Kingdom!

Chapter Twenty-One

CHRIST AND THE CHURCH

If we can accept the divine entry of God into human history through the man Jesus Christ, we cannot help accepting the unique nature of the fellowship which he founded. For in a true sense it is an extension of the actual visit, sustained by the living God. This explains the extraordinary strength and resilience of the Christian Church, and also why it is a mistake to regard it as a purely human organisation of those who happen to share the same religious views. Neither its own failures nor stupidities, neither the neglect nor the persecution of the surrounding world can ever destroy it. Sometimes outstandingly, but more often imperfectly, men and women all over the world have allowed something of the life, and therefore of the love, of God to invade their own personalities. Individually they are expendable, but as the agency of God they are indestructible. Maddening as this fact may be to the atheistic humanist, both past and present history confirm it over and over again.

For Jesus Christ himself began the vast project of establishing the Kingdom of God upon earth by calling together a handful of men. Before his own departure from the visible human scene he entrusted to these few the awe-inspiring task of telling the world about God and his Kingdom. He promised them supra-natural power, wisdom and love, and The Acts of the Apostles shows how this close-knit fellowship set out with joyful and hopeful audacity to build the Kingdom of Light in the Stygian darkness of the pagan world. These early Christians were held together by their common love for their Lord and his purpose, by their worship and their prayer. Violent persecution, public torture, social ostracism and dreadful forms of death could neither quench the fire nor defeat the purpose of the young Church. The movement proved unconquerable, and still proves unconquerable, because its unseen roots are in the eternal God.

Now it may seem a far cry indeed from that pristine, heroic fellowship to the Christians of today, who are too often tied by tradition and prejudice. Yet it remains true that wherever a church is sincerely dedicated to the living God and committed to the pattern of outgoing love, the same joyful certainty and the same paradox of vulnerable indestructibility continue to be exhibited. When we have made all the criticisms we can of those sections of the Church which are antiquated and backward-looking, we still have to reckon with the real builders of the Kingdom, who exist in every branch of the Christian Church. Having worked with and lived with such people for many years, I am ready to believe the truth of Paul's startling statement that Christians are 'the Body of Christ'.

The work of the Christian Church in the dark, fear-ridden parts of the world today is almost completely unknown to the ordinary man of goodwill. But anyone who takes the trouble to study what the churches are actually doing will see how they are proving to be the spearhead of good against centuries-old fear, superstition and prejudice. I believe the man of goodwill without much religious faith would be enormously impressed if he could realise what is being done by the Christian churches in works of human compassion alone. The true lover of humanity could not but feel deep sympathy with those Christians who are impelled by the love of God to serve fear-ridden and disease-stricken humanity in almost all parts of the world. But the man of goodwill takes, as a rule, not much more than a passing glance at the existing churches in this country. He sees readily enough the outmoded pieties and the undoubted pettiness of some Church members. But if he would penetrate further and seek the heart and soul of the whole matter, he would find in any true Christian fellowship that quality of compassionate love which is both inspired and sustained by the living God.

While it is true that the Christian Church has proved itself to be the spearhead of light in primitive pagan darkness, and indeed is still proving so today, its task in this country is not nearly so clear-cut. The true Christian sees with painful clarity the need for a recovery of a true religious faith, and many heroic efforts have been made, and are being made, to communicate it. I have already suggested that one of the Christian's urgent tasks is the giving of essential information, and I do not think that can be denied, but I am coming to believe more and more that the right 'way-in' in the prevailing atmosphere of today is to stress the need for compassionate service.

For although I do not doubt that some have found a religious faith in the mammoth evangelistic rallies which are held from time to time, I find it impossible to believe that this is ever going to be the way for a large-scale recovery of religious faith among ordinary people. The Englishman is basically sensible and practical, and although like anybody else he can be swept by superficial emotion for a time, his life is actually governed by much deeper emotions and affections. On the whole he is not 'spiritual' by nature at all, and unless 'faith' is expressed in actions which he can see and appreciate he is not likely to be convinced. Because of his unconscious but centuries-old impregnation by Christian belief, he often knows instinctively what is genuinely good and kind and unselfish, and on the whole he admires it. He may be a Pelagian,[1] but, to be blunt, no argument in the world is ever going to persuade him that a good man, however irreligious, goes to hell, or that a bad man, however religious, goes to heaven!

It seems to me that the re-presentation of Christianity in today's situation might well begin with a re-emphasis

[1] The heresy of the monk Pelagius was that he considered people to be fundamentally good rather than fundamentally evil.

of the teaching of Matthew 25, verses 31 to the end, to which I have already twice referred. It seems to me a most useful *argumentum ad hominem* with the strongest possible authority behind it. People have never been so aware of the dire distress of other human beings, and in this parable – the only recorded picture of the final judgment – we have an argument which appeals alike to the basic kindliness and powerful sense of justice which lie deep in the Anglo-Saxon character. For here we find the King categorically stating that the way in which we treat people, consciously or unconsciously, willingly or unwillingly, is the way in which we treat him. Here, in the ultimate issue, is no airy-fairy religious notion but downright practicality. If a man helps a fellow-man in need he is to that extent serving Christ. Inasmuch as he turns a blind eye or deaf ear to human need he is failing to serve Christ the King. It is as simple and as profound as that. Of course the moment we can get people to take such teaching seriously they find themselves confronted with their own prejudice, intolerance and lack of outgoing love. Indeed, they may well become aware that their real sin, as distinct from the 'sins' which they may or may not have committed, is a failure to love, a refusal to be committed, a dislike of being involved. Valuable as human love is, something is needed to deepen, enlarge and strengthen it. And here, I believe, is the point where men can come into contact with the living God. I do not mean merely that a man's own insufficiency of love drives him back upon the resources of God, although this is true, and such an experience has happened to many people. I mean that when a man whole-heartedly commits himself to the way of love, compassion and service, he finds that the pattern itself is surprisingly, and perhaps disconcertingly, alive. For the living Christ is really quite discoverable and no one recovers a true religious faith without a personal encounter with him.

We have now to face an unpleasant fact. It would be delightful indeed to imagine that all the nice, good, kind people would immediately become whole-hearted

Christians if only they were properly to grasp the true nature and purpose of the Christian faith. I believe this is true of a good many men and women of goodwill, who live in almost complete ignorance of what Christianity is all about, and that is why I have constantly stressed the need for Christian information. But there is a challenge and a demand made by the living Christ that many people would rather avoid. It is far easier to evade the moral responsibility which Christ may put upon one, by criticising the churches and satisfying the conscience by doing deeds of kindness, than to declare oneself boldly and unequivocally ready to serve the King. The unpleasant truth must be stated: some people deliberately avoid anything that may lead them to the divine encounter.

Further, it is significant that those who write of their experience of true conversion to the Christian faith always tell of a time of struggle. Their struggle is not with an historic fact, not with a philosophy of living, and not with any branch of the Church, but with the gently persistent, inexorable claim of Jesus Christ. The very bitterness of their attacks upon Christianity is later revealed to be only the measure of their fight against the one ultimate authority, the Son of God. Some of those whom we know to have had such experience (and there must be many thousands of whom there is no record) have found this penetrating, challenging spirit through contact with a group of true Christians, who were themselves probably quite unaware of issuing any challenge. Others, who have taken the trouble to read and study, have found to their alarm and discomfiture that what they thought was a safely distant historical figure becomes disconcertingly alive and contemporary.

But for every one who makes contact with a living Christian fellowship or studies the New Testament for himself there are thousands who do neither. They know nothing of the historic origin of Christianity, its present-day battles, or of the fundamental difference which the presence of Christ makes to so many people. If the churches were seen to be focal points of love and compassion, of understanding and service, if their services were known to be meetings of worship for those who are, or would like to be, agents of self-giving love, then at least the nice, friendly people without faith would know 'what religion is all about'. They might or might not accept the challenge to Christian living, but at least there would be the chance that the people of goodwill without faith might join forces with the people of goodwill with faith, to the very great spiritual benefit of all concerned.

Thus, I have come to believe that our best chance of creating the conditions for a spiritual revival lies in the repeated stressing of Christian humanism. Humanism without religion lacks depth, purpose and authority, but the humanism advocated by Jesus Christ seems to me peculiarly appropriate to our age. For even the least intelligent of people are beginning to see that unless they love and understand one another they will most certainly destroy one another. If the true nature and function of the Christian Church were rediscovered many might come to realise that only in the Kingdom of God, which is the Kingdom of Love, is there hope and strength, and the only possible security. For what ultimately matters is not religious exercises *per se* but the way in which we behave towards other people, our willingness or unwillingness to be involved in the vast purpose of love. The Anglo-Saxon may be suspicious of churchiness, of technical religious terms, of rites and robes, of bells and smells, which seem to him irrelevant to the business of living. But he is by no means unmoved by the needs of the handicapped and under-privileged, the homeless and the helpless, when he is made aware of them. It seems to me therefore that the most hopeful place in which to build a bridge between the worlds of faith and unfaith is on the common ground of human compassion.

I have written in this book about two worlds of goodwill which are known to me personally – the one whose compassion and love flow out of its faith in God, and the other which produces actions of compassion and self-giving service with little or no articulate religious faith. I am not for a moment suggesting that these are the only two worlds which exist in our country – there are vast fields of greed, stupidity, selfishness and fear, which lie quite outside the categories under consideration. No, what I am pleading for is that these two worlds, which are at present largely strangers to one another, might become one in spirit, a powerful army of true goodness and true love, following the pattern and inspired by the Spirit of the contemporary God. On the one hand the Church should welcome with open arms those who are plainly exhibiting the fruits of the Spirit, however sketchily and ill-informed their ideas of the Christian faith may be. On the other hand I would like to see the men and women of goodwill but little faith making a positive invasion of the churches, bringing with them their own insights, refusing to be dismayed by what appears to be outdated and irrelevant, and joining in what is the heart and soul of the matter, the worship of the living God and the expression of his love and purpose in everyday human life.

CONCLUSION

Many people of sensitivity and perception, whether they have a religious faith or not, view with dismay the growing materialism of this age. To anyone who is in the least alive to the contemporary God, the general life of our world, despite many virtues, exhibits all the symptoms of God-deficiency. For the present generation is, albeit unconsciously, attempting to prove that man *can* live by bread alone. 'The good life' is conceived almost entirely in terms of creature comforts, labour-saving appliances, better clothes, better and longer holidays, more money to spend and more leisure to enjoy. None of these things is wrong in itself. But when they are assumed to satisfy every desire, ambition and human aspiration, we are surely right to be alarmed at the grip of materialism. For when possessions, pleasures and the thought of physical security fill a man's horizon, he ceases to ask himself such basic questions as 'What am I?' or 'What am I here for?' He may gain the whole world, but he will lose his own soul.

Now I do not believe there is any remedy for this suffocating materialism except the recovery of a religious faith, and that means, above all, the recovery of true, essential Christianity. For it is only when it is plainly seen that life's great purpose is the building of the universal Kingdom of God, and that the object of human living is the development of the human spirit, that the irrelevance of such things as material success becomes apparent. Close contact with the living Spirit of the living God, whether it be by conventional religious approach or not, is the only thing that will reveal to us the lunatic topsy-turvydom of many of our current values. Without the Christian revelation, without a point of reference which lies beyond the present human situation, I cannot myself see that any really cogent argument can be advanced against materialism.

Man does not of course live by bread alone; he merely continues his physical existence with some concomitant mental phenomena. It is the authentic Word of God, the supra-human truth which challenges him and brings his spirit to life. Sooner or later, if people will only pursue their thoughts far enough, they must see that life without a true faith is quite literally a dead loss. At present the religious instinct, which I believe to exist in everyone is being perverted. All naturally worship someone or something, but in the commonly assumed absence of God, this worship is given almost wholly to such things as success, sport, the heroes or heroines of the fantasy-world of the screen or stage, or to the mysteries of science. Such a superstition as astrology may flourish as a substitute-religion, while some fancy version of an Eastern religion may attract the intellectual agnostic. But perversions of the instinct to worship God do not in the long run rescue man either from his own solitariness or from the closed-system of materialism. The way out, paradoxically enough, lies in no form of uncommitted escapism, but in a closer commitment to life. Christianity shows the way of such closer commitment; it does not merely restore a man's faith in God but inevitably involves him in compassion and service. This is both the strength and the difficulty about the Christian way of life. Other methods may give 'religious' experiences, but only Christianity insists that the life of the spirit must be expressed within the terms of the present human predicament. That is why only Christianity can fully satisfy the desire to worship and the desire to serve. It is demonstrably true that when people begin to love their neighbours as themselves, to experience and to express compassion for those in all kinds of human need, they become spiritually alive.

In Christ's teaching enormous stress is laid upon the

way in which men and women treat each other, and the whole concept of a human being is raised in value because he is declared to be a loved and valued child of God. The relief of human suffering, of whatever kind, the liberation of human beings from fear, ignorance and evil, the compassionate use of human talents and personality – all these are shown to be of the highest importance. For they are expressions of the divine purpose as well as the means of developing the human spirit. But because we are infected personally, nationally and internationally with the prideful spirit of competitiveness, we have got our priorities hopelessly mixed, and cannot see the truth. Most people admire compassion from a safe distance, and applaud good works which do not involve them personally. But willing compassionate involvement in dark and difficult human problems stands very low in the list of most people's plans and ambitions. In our modern world we have come to accept it as commonplace that the launching of a single small satellite should cost more than the building and equipping of a modern hospital. We find it easier to be fascinated by the possibilities of space-travel than to be distressed by the plight of millions of refugees living in misery on our own planet. Real Christianity is good bread-and-butter stuff which nourishes men's souls by the worship of the true God and by the exercise of practical compassion. But the fascination of modern technical advances in every department of our physical life has made us like spoiled children who long for sweets and more sweets, and have lost their stomach for truly nourishing food.

At the risk of being repetitious, I must say once more that I believe that only a new grasp of Christian humanism can save us from the subtle deteriorations of materialism. Goodwill, kind-heartedness, self-sacrifice and the willingness to serve are, of course, good, but they are absorbed in the desert of material godlessness unless they are joined to a supra-natural purpose and reinforced by a supra-natural power. And this is exactly what the Christian Church should be. For any army of men and women who are conscious, despite their own defects, of co-operating with the Mind and purpose which began, and will end, the human scene, cannot be lightly dismissed as a crowd of 'do-gooders'.

Whenever the Christian Church has in fact been such a dedicated fellowship, it has often met with hostility, ridicule and persecution, but it has never been disregarded. At this present time the Church is taken very seriously in former-Communist countries, and hardly ever looked upon as a mere hangover from a superstitious past. For the men with hard faces, the men who lust for power and see their fellows as no more than units in a machine, know intuitively that the Church is the implacable champion of human liberty, of the truly human values and the finest human aspirations. Recent history shows quite clearly that when the conflict becomes acute in a totalitarian society it is the Christian Church which alone can successfully stand up for human liberty and conscience. It should be remembered that it was not the well-meaning agnostics who were able to defy Hitler but the Christian churches. Today it is not the vague humanist who is regarded as the enemy of Communism; it is the Christian, who has standards and loyalties which are rooted in God.

I think something else should be said. If we were able to conduct a survey of those human beings who are giving the most devoted service to people in need, whether it is to the blind, the deaf and dumb, the leper, the spastic or any other of our afflicted fellow human beings, I am confident that we should find the Christians in the majority. I believe ordinary men and women would be amazed if they could see how often, in the black spots of the world's superstition, ignorance, disease and fear, the Christians were the first to arrive. There are, to my knowledge, many thousands of dedicated Christian men and women who are day after day mediating the love of God despite every difficulty and discouragement.

Now in this country of traditional Christian values, a land

which may well lead the world in matters of justice and liberty, it is very easy to underestimate the powers of evil. The issues are blurred, and the battle between good and evil is scarcely recognised by the majority of people. We know nothing at first-hand of the cruelty of dictatorship. We rarely have to suffer much for our faith, if indeed we have one. But how much longer this atmosphere of comfortable apathy is going to last is anybody's guess. Already we have a generation growing up without moral standards, with no sense of purpose and with little, if any, concern for the enormous human problems which are coming to light all over the world. Mere 'kindness', 'niceness', 'goodwill', or 'tolerance' are never going to supply a dynamic for living, a cause for which to live and die, or a purpose commanding a person's total dedication. We who are middle-aged may have jogged along, content with those liberal humanist values left to us by preceding ages of faith. But nothing less than the recovery of real Christianity, with its ineradicable emphasis upon human compassion, and its inexorable insistence upon the transience of this world and the reality of eternity, will ever put back into the disillusioned the faith, hope, courage and gaiety which are the marks of a human being co-operating with his Creator.

I believe it to be essential for us to recover the dimension of eternity if we are to value this life properly and live it with sanity and courage. The pieties of former ages cannot satisfy the modern mind. For example, the conception of 'eternity' as merely endless aeons of time has given many people an idea of 'Heaven' which they have rejected as absurd. But surely here the conception of another 'dimension' can come to the aid of our thought. No thinking Christian today believes in 'Heaven' or 'everlasting life' as a mere extension of time-and-space existence, however purified and exalted! He believes that after the death of the body there is a release from the time-and-space predicament and a conscious sharing in the timeless Life of God, in which there are probably various stages of enlightenment and knowledge. There may be no words to describe such a timeless state, but that proves no more than that its reality is beyond present human expression. Yet it remains the unshakable conviction of Christians, from New Testament days until today, that there is what must be called, for want of a better word, an 'eternal' order, an 'eternal' plan and an 'eternal' life. Compared with these eternal verities the present human scene gives no more than a hint of unimagined realities.

The trend of modern thought, with its concentration upon making the most of this present life and the tacit assumption that death means extinction, makes it particularly easy for people to disbelieve in, or to ridicule, life after death. But historically, it is the conviction of unseen realities which has given men and women invincible strength. There might be some truth in the old gibe of pie-in-the-sky if we found all Christians doing absolutely nothing to better the world, on the grounds that they have Heaven to look forward to; and all the atheists working like mad to relieve every form of human distress, since this life is all that we have! But that is obviously and demonstrably untrue, and something very like the reverse is sometimes the case. It is those who are in touch with the eternal order who make the most heroic and sustained efforts to improve conditions for their fellows. It is those who know God to be eternal who most satisfactorily prove that God is their contemporary.